To:

_____

From:

_____

God Always Keeps His Promises

Unshakable Hope for Kids

MAX LUCADO

ADAPTED BY TAMA FORTNER

Illustrated by Alessia Trunfio

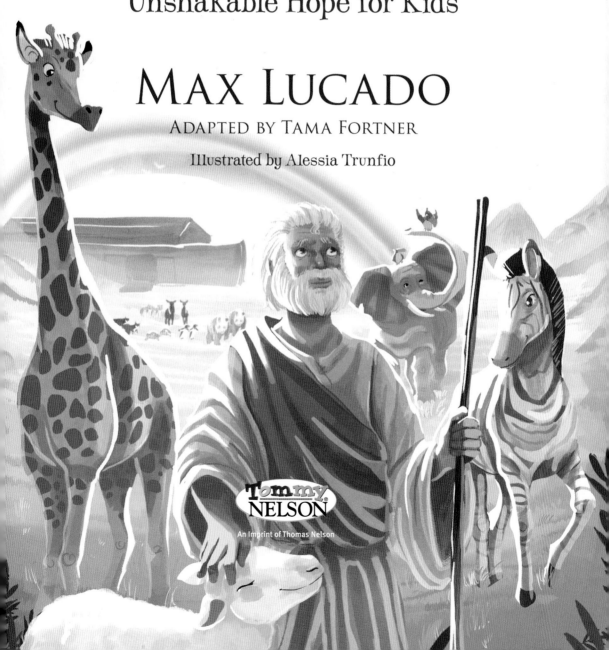

Tommy
NELSON®

An Imprint of Thomas Nelson

Published in Nashville, Tennessee, by Tommy Nelson. Tommy Nelson is an imprint of Thomas Nelson. Thomas Nelson is a registered trademark of HarperCollins Christian Publishing, Inc.

Illustrated by Alessia Trunfio.

Tommy Nelson titles may be purchased in bulk for educational, business, fund-raising, or sales promotional use. For information, please e-mail SpecialMarkets@ThomasNelson.com.

Unless otherwise noted, Scripture quotations are taken from the International Children's Bible®. Copyright © 1986, 1988, 1999, 2015 by Thomas Nelson. Used by permission. All rights reserved.

Scripture quotations marked ESV are from the ESV® Bible (The Holy Bible, English Standard Version®). Copyright © 2001 by Crossway, a publishing ministry of Good News Publishers. Used by permission. All rights reserved.

Scripture quotations marked MSG are from *The Message.* Copyright © by Eugene H. Peterson 1993, 1994, 1995, 1996, 2000, 2001, 2002. Used by permission of Tyndale House Publishers, Inc.

Scripture quotations marked NCV are from the New Century Version®. © 2005 by Thomas Nelson. Used by permission. All rights reserved.

Scripture quotations marked NIV are from the Holy Bible, New International Version®, NIV®. Copyright © 1973, 1978, 1984, 2011 by Biblica, Inc.® Used by permission of Zondervan. All rights reserved worldwide. www.zondervan.com. The "NIV" and "New International Version" are trademarks registered in the United States Patent and Trademark Office by Biblica, Inc.®

Scripture quotations marked NLT are from the Holy Bible, New Living Translation. © 1996, 2004, 2007, 2013, 2015 by Tyndale House Foundation. Used by permission of Tyndale House Publishers, Inc., Carol Stream, Illinois 60188. All rights reserved.

ISBN 978-1-4003-1687-8

Library of Congress Cataloging-in-Publication Data

Names: Lucado, Max, author. | Fortner, Tama, 1969- adapter. | Trunfio, Alessia, illustrator.
Title: God always keeps his promises : unshakable hope for kids / Max Lucado; adapted by Tama Fortner ; illustrated by Alessia Trunfio.
Description: Nashville : Thomas Nelson, 2018. |
Identifiers: LCCN 2017057154 (print) | LCCN 2018010244 (ebook) | ISBN 9781400316885 (e-book) | ISBN 9781400316878 (padded hardcover)
Subjects: LCSH: God (Christianity)--Promises--Juvenile literature. | Trust in God (Christianity)--Juvenile literature. | Hope—Religious aspects--Christianity--Juvenile literature.
Classification: LCC BS680.P68 (ebook) | LCC BS680.P68 L825 2018 (print) | DDC 242/.62--dc23
LC record available at https://lccn.loc.gov/2017057154

Printed in China

18 19 20 21 22 DSC 6 5 4 3 2 1

Mfr: DSC / Shenzhen, China / July 2018 / PO #9475421

Denalyn and I happily dedicate this book to our grandson
Max Wesley Bishop
May you build your life on the promises of God.

Contents

A Letter to Parents

"I promise." We hear those words early and often in life.

"I'll be home early. I promise."

"We'll play next weekend. I promise."

"You can visit me this summer. I promise."

People make promises. And for the most part, people intend to keep their promises. But we are not on this earth for long before we learn that not everyone can. Not everyone does. Promises get broken. And consequently, hearts get broken. We tend to grow cynical, distrustful, and jaded. We wonder, *Does anyone keep their word?*

God does. The Bible contains well over seven thousand promises. God is a promise maker, and God is a promise keeper. If He says it, we can believe it.

Your children need to know this. No one, including the child you love, will get through life pain-free. We all feel the sting of a broken promise. So teach them to trust in God's Word. Acquaint them with His great and powerful promises. Urge them not to stand on the pain in life or the problems of life but to stand on the great and precious promises of God.

They'll be glad you did. I promise.

—Max Lucado

CHAPTER 1

GOD'S PROMISE FOR YOU

God Will Make You Like Jesus

God said, "Let us make human beings in our image and likeness."

—GENESIS 1:26

Has anyone ever said you "take after" your mom or your dad? "Take after" means that you look like someone else. For example, you might have your mom's eyes, your dad's ears, or your great-uncle Alfred's freckled nose and flaming red hair!

There's Someone else you "take after" too. *God.* That's because you are created in His image. He made you to be like Him. Not to be a god, but to be a *child of God* who loves and gives and helps like Him. He even sent His Son, Jesus, to show you how. And each day, God works to make you just a little bit more like His perfect Son.

Out of all the amazing things God created, only people were made in His image. Not the oceans, not the birds, not the chimpanzees. Only people were made in God's image.

So if you ever wonder who you really are, remember this wonderful promise: you are made in the image of God. You are His idea. His child. You "take after" Him. And as you learn to love Him, He'll make you more and more like His Son.

God had had a busy week.

He had taken a whole lot of nothing and created . . . well . . . a whole lot of everything. And with just a few words! He spoke, and light shot across the skies. Oceans and mountains, rivers and seas, plants and trees—all were created when He spoke. At God's command, eagles soared, whales sang, and lions roared.

Yes, God had been busy. And He wasn't finished yet!

God stooped down and scooped up a mound of dust. Like a potter shaping clay, He began to work. He made eyes to see, ears to hear, and a mouth to smile. He added hands to help, a mind to think, and a heart to love. And when everything was just as He wanted it to be, God leaned down just a little bit more and breathed life into His creation. This was the first man, and he was called Adam.

Adam's first job was to name all the animals. Just imagine! Did they all wait quietly in a line? Or did Adam have to chase them around, climbing up trees and peeking under bushes?

And the names! How did Adam think of them all? Did he start with *A* and work his way to *Z*? "Hmm . . . that one with the funny nose I'll call *aardvark*." Then came *bat* and *cat*, followed by *donkey, elephant*, and *falcon*. "And you over there with the long, long neck? *Giraffe* is the name for you."

But out of all the animals—from aardvark to zebra—Adam didn't find a helper that was just right for him.

So God made Adam fall into a deep, deep sleep. He took one of Adam's ribs and used it to make one last creation: woman. God brought her to Adam, and she was called Eve.

Adam and Eve were unlike anything else God had made. They were created in His image, to be like Him. To give, to help, and to love like Him.

Do you ever feel small? Or not very important? It happens sometimes—when other kids make fun of you, when you're different, or when you mess up or make a mistake. If you ever find yourself wondering who you are or if you really matter, remember this beautiful promise from God: you are His child, made in His image, and you are worth everything to Him.

Of course, you aren't perfect! But God promises to keep working on you, every day making you just a little bit more like His perfect Son, Jesus. A little more loving, a little more giving, a little kinder too.

And that promise isn't just for you. Every person is God's beloved creation—no matter who they are, where they live, or what they have or do. So if you ever get angry or upset with someone, remember that God is working on that person too.

Everywhere you go and in everything you do, remember God's promise to you. You are His child. His idea. Created in His image. And . . .

He will make you more like Jesus.

MY PROMISE TO GOD

I will trust God to teach me to be more like Jesus.

Dear God, when this world tells me I'm nobody important, remind me that I am Your child—very loved and very important to You! Amen.

Lord, you are our father. We are like clay, and you
are the potter. Your hands made us all.

—ISAIAH 64:8

———✳———

You have begun to live the new life. In your new life you are
being made new. You are becoming like the One who made
you. This new life brings you the true knowledge of God.

—COLOSSIANS 3:10

———✳———

You made me and formed me with your hands. Give me
understanding so I can learn your commands.

—PSALM 119:73

———✳———

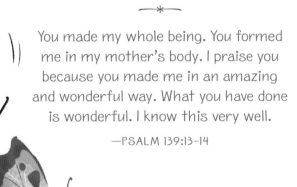

You made my whole being. You formed
me in my mother's body. I praise you
because you made me in an amazing
and wonderful way. What you have done
is wonderful. I know this very well.

—PSALM 139:13-14

CHAPTER 2

God Will Win the Battle

The God who
brings peace
will soon defeat
Satan and give
you power
over him.

—ROMANS 16:20

Do some days feel like you're fighting a battle? You try to do what's right, but it's just so hard! It's like there's someone fighting against you, trying to trick you into doing things you know you shouldn't do—like snatching that game from your sister or fibbing to your mom to get out of trouble.

Well . . . someone *is* out to trick you. His name is Satan, but he goes by some other names too. Like "Devil" and "father of lies." He's the ultimate villain, the crookedest crook, and the baddest of bad guys. And he's only got one mission in mind: to make God's children lose in their battle to do what's right.

But God gives you a promise for this fight: in the end, it's the Devil who will lose. No, that doesn't stop him from fighting. After all, the Devil has been at it a really long time—since Adam and Eve. But always remember this: the days may be tough and the fight may be terrible, but God will win.

It was a beautiful day in the garden. Adam and Eve wandered among the trees. They nibbled on berries and scratched the elephant behind its ear.

God had given them a fresh, new world. And everything in it was good.

Except the snake.

Of course, this was no ordinary snake. This was that sneaky old Devil himself.

He hid in the trees and waited to spring his trap. When Eve passed by, he called out, "Did God *really* say you can't eat *any* fruit from *any* tree?"

"No, we can eat any fruit," Eve said, "except fruit from the tree in the middle of the garden. If we even touch that fruit, we'll die!"

(Actually, God didn't say they couldn't even *touch* it, but Eve wasn't taking any chances!)

"You won't die," the snake hissed out a lie. "It'll make you as wise as God. God just doesn't want you to be as smart as He is."

Eve looked at the snake and then at the fruit. It *did* look delicious. And she wouldn't mind being as wise as God.

So she picked a piece. She sniffed it, and her mouth watered. Then she closed her eyes and took a bite. Still chewing, she gave it to Adam, and he took a bite too.

They had done the one thing God said they must not do.

At once, everything changed. There was definitely a chill in the air. Adam and Eve suddenly saw that they were naked! Snatching up fig leaves, they quickly started sewing. Just as they were putting the finishing touches on their leafy new wardrobe, they heard something. Or rather, Someone. *God!* He was walking in the garden.

Adam and Eve ran to hide.

"Adam?" God called. "Where are you?"

Adam gulped. "I was afraid because I'm naked," he said, "so I hid."

"Who told you that you were naked?" God asked. "Did you eat the fruit I told you not to eat?"

Of course, God already knew the answer. He also knew that snaky sneak Satan had tempted them to do it. Adam blamed Eve, and Eve blamed the snake. But God punished them all. From that day forward, sin, sickness, and even death came into the world. And Satan would forever be the Enemy of God's people.

But something else happened that day too. God gave His people a promise: The Devil will lose. No matter how much he lies or how hard he fights. God—and those who trust in Him—will win.

You may not know this, but you're a soldier. And every day you fight in a battle. It's a battle between good and evil.

The thing about battles is that it's important to know who your enemy is. To know what he wants and how he fights. Your Enemy is the Devil. His weapons are lies and tricks and temptations. He makes good things look bad and bad things look good. And he wants you to think you are all alone in this fight, that God isn't there for you, that He isn't even real. But that is a lie!

The truth is that God never leaves you to fight this battle alone. He fights right beside you. And He gives you a special armor too—the armor of His promises. One of those promises is about how the battle will end: the Devil is going to lose.

God will win the battle.

Though the Devil will try to trick and trap me, I will trust God to fight for me—and win!

Dear God, I know the Devil is real, but I also know You are bigger and stronger than he is. I will trust You to fight for me. Amen.

My dear children, you belong to God. So you have
defeated them because God's Spirit, who is in you,
is greater than the devil, who is in the world.

—1 JOHN 4:4

———✳———

Give yourselves to God. Stand against the devil,
and the devil will run away from you.

—JAMES 4:7

———✳———

Our fight is not against people on earth. We are fighting
against the rulers and authorities and the powers
of this world's darkness. We are fighting against the
spiritual powers of evil in the heavenly world.

—EPHESIANS 6:12

CHAPTER 3

GOD'S PROMISE FOR YOU

God Will Take Care of His People

"When you go
through deep waters,
I will be with you.
When you go through
rivers of difficulty,
you will not drown."

—ISAIAH 43:2 NLT

Trouble comes in all shapes and sizes. There's big trouble and little trouble and every size in between. You never know when or where trouble might pop up. But there is one thing you can be sure of: trouble is coming.

There's one more thing you can also be sure of: God is coming too.

Just think about Noah. Trouble was coming for Noah. Big trouble. In fact, everything about the story of Noah is big. A big boat—longer than a football field! A big job—not just building that boat but also taking care of all those animals. And a big flood—so big that it would cover even the mountaintops! But an even bigger God was coming too. Because God takes care of His people.

There's a promise in Noah's story—and not just the promise of the rainbow. It's the promise God first gave Noah. And it's one He gives to you too: trouble is coming, but God is coming too.

Noah stared at the ark. It was big. Bigger than big. It was huge!

God had told him to build it, so he did. For years Noah and his family chopped and sawed and hammered to build this gigantic boat called an ark.

And, oh, how the people had laughed. "Rain?" they scoffed. "A flood? Whoever heard of such a thing?" They shook their heads and went right back to their own lives. Lives filled with wickedness. It was because of that wickedness that God told Noah to build the boat.

And Noah always tried to do what God told him to do.

Now the ark was finished, and Noah stood looking up at it, while all around him, noise filled the air. Barking and braying. Hissing and honking. Roaring and squawking. Noah had never seen so many animals, and they were all waiting for him to lead them into the ark. Rhinos and hippos and mosquitos. (If only those bugs had been forgotten!) Elephants and eagles, geckos and giraffes, rabbits and reindeer. The place was a zoo!

And don't forget the food! Hay for the horses, nuts for the squirrels, and bunches of bananas for the monkeys.

God had given Noah a big job: build a big boat and fill it with a big bunch of animals. Because a big flood was coming. But God also gave Noah a big promise: He would keep Noah and his family safe.

As Noah loaded the last of the animals into the ark, clouds began to swirl. The sky grew dark, and the first little pitter-patter of raindrops fell.

So this is rain, Noah thought. He'd never seen it before. He took one last look at the world before he hurried into the ark, and God closed the door.

For forty days and nights, it rained. Those first few drops quickly turned into a raging, roaring flood that swallowed up the land, the trees, and even the mountaintops. Every living thing on earth was destroyed.

Everything except Noah, his family, and the animals on the ark.

After forty days of storms and months of floating, the boat landed with a bump on dry land. But more weeks passed before God said it was safe to leave the ark.

At last, Noah and his family stepped outside. The animals followed close behind, blinking in the bright sunshine. Everything was fresh and new and green.

Though the flood had been terrible, Noah, his family, and all the animals from the ark were safe. God had kept His promise. He had taken care of Noah. Just as He'd said He would.

Noah was facing trouble. Big trouble! A flood was coming that would destroy every living thing on earth. But God gave Noah a way to escape. A way to stay safe. Because God takes care of His people.

You may not realize this, but you are facing trouble too. A great big, gigantic flood of trouble. It's called sin, and everyone has it in their lives. Yes, even you. No matter how good you may try to be, sin sneaks in. It destroys people just like a flood does. But God gives you a way to escape. A way to stay safe and to stay close to Him. That way is Jesus—He's kind of like our boat. He saves us from the flood of sin. All you have to do is believe and obey Him.

That's the promise God gives you and everyone who chooses to love Him: trouble is coming, but God is coming too. Because . . .

God takes care of His people.

MY PROMISE TO GOD

I will trust God to take care of me and save me.

Dear God, thank You for sending Jesus to rescue me. Please take away all my sins and make my heart clean again. Amen.

It was by faith Noah heard God's warnings about things that he could not yet see. He obeyed God and built a large boat to save his family.

—HEBREWS 11:7

———✳———

All people have sinned and are not good enough for God's glory. People are made right with God by his grace, which is a free gift. They are made right with God by being made free from sin through Jesus Christ.

—ROMANS 3:23–24

———✳———

If we claim we have no sin, we are only fooling ourselves and not living in the truth. But if we confess our sins to him, he is faithful and just to forgive us our sins and to cleanse us from all wickedness.

—1 JOHN 1:8–9 NLT

———✳———

Noah did everything just as God commanded him.

—GENESIS 6:22 NIV

———✳———

"God loved the world so much that he gave his only Son. God gave his Son so that whoever believes in him may not be lost, but have eternal life."

—JOHN 3:16

———✳———

Christ Jesus came into the world to save sinners.

—1 TIMOTHY 1:15

———✳———

Christ died for us while we were still sinners. In this way God shows his great love for us.

—ROMANS 5:8

CHAPTER 4

God Will Forgive You

Abram believed the
Lord. And the Lord
accepted Abram's
faith, and that
faith made him
right with God.

—GENESIS 15:6

You've probably heard people say things like, "Just have faith." But what is *faith*? And how do you have it?

The Bible says faith is believing something is real, even if you don't see it (Hebrews 11:1). There are things in the world that you believe in, even though you can't see them, like wind or gravity or love. You can't see those things, but you know they're real. You have *faith* that they are real.

Faith in God then means believing God is real, even though you can't see Him. It's also believing that God will keep His promises and *living* like you believe those promises. Like Noah, who built an ark before it ever rained a drop. Like Peter, who stepped out of the boat and onto the lake to walk to Jesus. And Abram, who believed God would do what He said He would do—no matter how impossible it seemed.

from Genesis 12–18, 21

Abram was an ordinary man living an ordinary life. Until God spoke to him.

"Go," God said. "I'm not going to tell you where, but I'll show you the way. And when you get there, I will bless you and make your family into a great nation."

God was offering Abram everything. And what did He want in return? *Faith*. God wanted Abram to believe He would do what He said He would do.

Of course, Abram could have said no. He could have said, "I'd like a map, please." He could have asked, "What exactly is Your plan, Lord?" But he didn't. Abram had faith. So he went. With his camels, his donkeys, and his servants. With his wife, Sarai. But without any children, because they didn't have any.

Abram traveled through cities and deserts. He wasn't perfect. He made mistakes. But He kept going, trusting God to show him the way.

At last they reached the land of Canaan, and God said, "Look all around you. I'm giving everything you can see to you, to your children, and to your children's children forever. Your family will be like the dust of the ground—too many to count."

What an amazing promise! But there was a problem. Abram and Sarai didn't have any children. Not one. And they were old. *Really old*. God was promising them the impossible. Still, Abram trusted God to do what He said He would do.

Years passed, and there was still no baby. So, one night, God led Abram outside and reminded him of His promise. "Do you see all those stars?" God asked. "One day, your family will be like those stars. You won't be able to count them all."

Abram believed God would keep His promise. He had faith.

Still more years passed and God came to remind Abram once again of His promise: "I will make you the father of many nations." Then God changed Abram's name to *Abraham*, which means "father of many."

Sarai became *Sarah*, and God promised her a son. Which made Sarah laugh—after all, she was ninety years old! And Abraham was ninety-nine! How could she have a baby now? It was impossible!

But just a year later, Sarah was laughing again. This time, she laughed with joy as she and Abraham held their baby son, Isaac. God had kept His promise. Because God always does what He says He will do.

Abraham had faith. He believed God's promise to bless every nation on earth through a family he was far too old to have.

And remember, Abraham didn't have the Bible or its stories of faith like we have. Abraham simply believed that God would do what He said He would do. He had *faith*. And that faith made him right with God.

When you believe God's promises—when you have faith—you are also made right with God. Your sins are forgiven and forgotten. And *you* become one of the shining stars in God's family. Because God always keeps His promises. Just as He kept His promise to Abraham, God's promises are true for you. God will do what He says He will do.

When you have faith, God will forgive you.

MY PROMISE TO GOD

I trust God to do what He says He will do: He will forgive me because I have faith in Him.

Dear God, I trust You. Help me to believe Your promises and to follow You like Abraham did. Amen.

The One who called you is completely
dependable. If he said it, he'll do it!

—I THESSALONIANS 5:24 MSG

———✳———

God's way of making people right with him begins and
ends with faith. As the Scripture says, "The person who
is made right with God by faith will live forever."

—ROMANS 1:17

———✳———

People receive God's promise by having faith. . . . All of
Abraham's children can have that promise. . . . It is
for anyone who lives with faith like Abraham.

—ROMANS 4:16

———✳———

Without faith no one can please God. Anyone who
comes to God must believe that he is real and that
he rewards those who truly want to find him.

—HEBREWS 11:6

CHAPTER 5

GOD'S PROMISE FOR YOU

God Will Make Everything Work for Good

"I'll see to it
that everything
works out for
the best."

—ISAIAH 54:17 MSG

Have you ever thought that life is just not fair? You try your best to do what God says is right, but things still go wrong. And then there are those people who don't even care about God or doing what's right, and their lives seem trouble free. It's just not fair!

When life isn't fair, God gives you a promise: He'll use your troubles for good. Somehow. Some way. Just ask Joseph.

If there's one person in the Bible who understood that life isn't fair, it was Joseph. He went from being the prince of his family to the bottom of a pit. His own brothers sold him as a slave, but he still tried to do right. Alone, far from home, and with more troubles than he could count, Joseph trusted God, and God used his troubles to do a very great good.

Joseph sighed and stared at the prison walls. His cell was dark and damp and smelly. Rats *scritch-scratched* across the floor. No windows, no sunshine, and no way out.

It wasn't fair! He didn't belong here! He hadn't done anything wrong! Joseph tried not to be angry. He trusted God. So he did his best and tried to do what was right. Even though he had been treated poorly by his brothers. Even though he was in prison for a crime he did not commit.

Just a few days ago, he thought he'd found a way out at last. Two men from Pharaoh's court—a baker and a butler—were thrown into the prison. They were both having terrible dreams. Joseph offered to help. He knew God would tell him what their dreams meant.

It was bad news for the baker. "Get your life in order," Joseph warned. "You're about to die." But it was good news for the butler. "Pack your bags. You're going back to Pharaoh. And while you're there, could you tell him about me?" Joseph asked.

The butler promised he would. But he didn't. He forgot all about Joseph.

Joseph had been wronged yet again. Even in prison, Joseph did his best. He made his bed, made friends, and made a good impression on the warden, who put him in charge of the other prisoners.

For two years, Joseph stared at those prison doors, praying they would open. Two years is a very long time to wait. Finally, one day, everything changed.

Pharaoh had a dream, and the butler *finally* remembered Joseph, the man who could tell them what dreams meant. And—faster than you can say *pretty please*—Joseph went from prison to palace. When Joseph said Pharaoh's dreams meant a terrible famine was coming, Pharaoh put Joseph in charge of storing all the food in Egypt. When the surrounding countries had no food, Egypt had plenty. God had used Joseph's trials for good. Many people didn't starve because of Joseph. And it wasn't long before Joseph's brothers came begging for some of that food.

Joseph watched his brothers tremble in fear. This was his chance to get even. He could toss those no-good brothers of his into a pit, like they'd done to him. But he didn't. Instead, he said, "You meant to hurt me, but God turned your evil into good. And the lives of many people were saved."

Through all his troubles, Joseph trusted God. And God worked everything out for good.

Do you ever wonder *why*? Why was Joseph in prison? Why are there bullies and diseases and storms? Why do bad things happen to good people and good things happen to bad people? Doesn't God care?

Yes, God cares! Remember, God is the One who counts every sparrow and feeds every tiny bird. And you're so much more important to Him than any bird (Matthew 6:26, 10:29). God is working in every moment of your life—the good ones and the not-so-good ones. He cares about everything that happens to you. That's why God gives you this promise: He will make everything work out for good.

God won't let evil win. Instead, He'll take your tough times and troubles—even the evil things people plan against you—and He'll use them to do good. He did it for Joseph, and He'll do it for you too.

Until He does, do what Joseph did. Trust. Wait. Pray. Believe. And keep following Him. Because when the time is just right . . .

God will make everything work out for good.

MY PROMISE TO GOD

I will trust God, even when things do not seem fair, when I am waiting, or when I am hurting. I will believe that in the end, God will make things work out for good.

Dear God, it's hard for me to understand why bad things happen. But when they do, help me to trust You—and to look for the good You will bring out of them. Amen.

We know that in everything God works for
the good of those who love him.

—ROMANS 8:28

"As the heavens are higher than the earth, so are my ways
higher than your ways and my thoughts than your thoughts."

—ISAIAH 55:9 NIV

Trust the Lord with all your heart. Don't depend
on your own understanding. Remember the Lord in
everything you do. And he will give you success.

—PROVERBS 3:5–6

God's voice thunders in wonderful ways. He does
great things we cannot understand.

—JOB 37:5

God certainly does everything at just the right time. But
we can never completely understand what he is doing.

—ECCLESIASTES 3:11

CHAPTER 6

GOD'S PROMISE FOR YOU

God's Word Will Show You the Way

I will instruct
you and teach
you in the way
you should go.

—PSALM 32:8 NIV

What's the most amazing thing you have ever seen? Perhaps it was something huge, like the endless waves of an ocean or a soaring mountain. Perhaps it was something smaller and closer to home, like a rainbow after a storm.

Life is full of wonderful things to see. But if there were ever anyone whose life was filled with amazing sights, it was Moses. There was that burning bush that never burned up. Then the ten plagues. Just imagine all those hopping frogs. Pharaoh saw them and almost croaked! There was the day the Red Sea opened and closed up again. Manna from heaven, feasts of quail, and water pouring from a rock.

But perhaps the most incredible thing Moses ever saw was God's first written message to His people. It was a promise, written in stone, that would show God's people the way to Him and the way to heaven. And Moses saw it first.

from Exodus 19–20, 24, 31–34

Moses stopped climbing. He stroked his long beard and leaned on his staff. It was the same staff that had turned into a snake and that God had used to part the Red Sea. *Halfway there*, he thought. *Halfway up this mountain*.

It had been three months since the Israelites left Egypt. Three months of whining and complaining and marching through the desert. God had led them here, to the bottom of Mount Sinai. And then He had told Moses He was coming to speak to His people.

For three days, the people washed and scrubbed. Then they waited for God.

Suddenly, a thick cloud covered the mountain. Lightning flashed, thunder boomed, and a long, loud trumpet blast cut through the air. The mountain shook, and smoke rose up as if it were on fire. Then the Lord began to speak. He told His people how He wanted them to live. And He promised that if they would obey Him, they would be His chosen people.

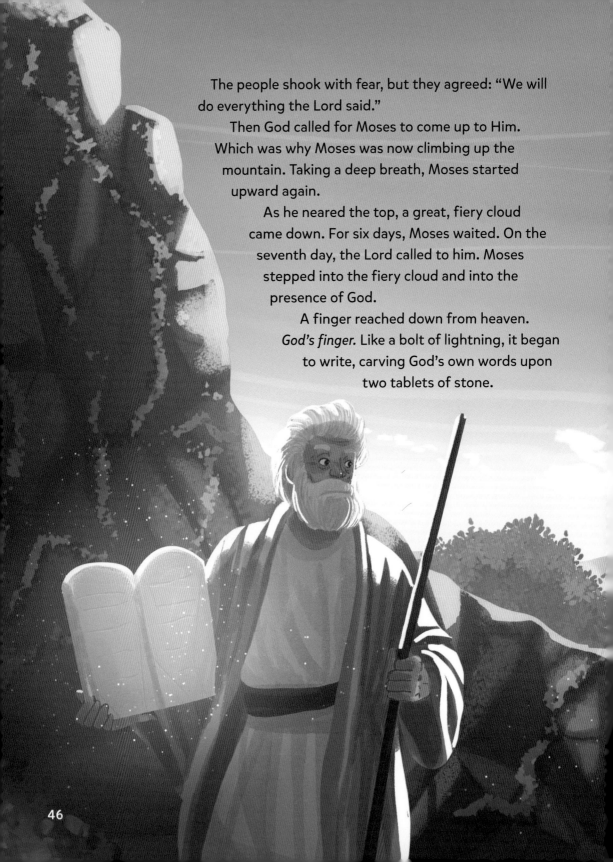

The people shook with fear, but they agreed: "We will do everything the Lord said."

Then God called for Moses to come up to Him. Which was why Moses was now climbing up the mountain. Taking a deep breath, Moses started upward again.

As he neared the top, a great, fiery cloud came down. For six days, Moses waited. On the seventh day, the Lord called to him. Moses stepped into the fiery cloud and into the presence of God.

A finger reached down from heaven. *God's finger.* Like a bolt of lightning, it began to write, carving God's own words upon two tablets of stone.

When the Lord finished, He gave the tablets to Moses. On them were the first of God's written instructions to His people. Ten Commandments—ten laws that told His people how to live, how to love each other, and how to love God.

The people promised to follow God's laws. Sometimes they did, but often they did not. It was just so hard to obey each one perfectly. That's why God sent His Son.

Many years after God first wrote His laws on those tablets of stone, Jesus came to *show* His people how to live, how to love each other, and how to love God. And He came so they could be forgiven when they didn't do it perfectly.

The words of Jesus and the stories of all He did were also written down. We still have those words and stories today. They are called the New Testament. Together with God's Words of the Old Testament, they make up the Bible—God's gift to us. That gift gives us a promise: to show us the way to forgiveness . . . to heaven . . . to God.

When God carved His Ten Commandments on those two stone tablets, it was a first for Him. Before this, God simply spoke. In the beginning, He spoke and stars burst into the heavens. He talked to Adam and Eve about the one fruit they shouldn't eat. He chatted with Noah about building a boat. And He told Abram not to worry about a map, just go. But when God carved His commandments onto those tablets of stone, it was the first time He *wrote* to His people.

And what a gift! The beauty of God's written Word—whether it's on those tablets of stone or in the Holy Bible we have today—is that everyone can read it. People who have never heard the voice of God can know the words of God. That's so very important because there's a promise in those words. A promise of hope for all people. A promise for *you.* When you want to know how to live and how to get to heaven . . .

God's Word will show you the way.

MY PROMISE TO GOD

I believe the Bible is filled with God's own words. And I believe His words will show me the way to heaven and to Him.

Dear Lord, fill my heart with a love for Your Word. Use it to teach me how to love others and how to love You. Amen.

All Scripture is inspired by God and is useful for teaching and for showing people what is wrong in their lives. It is useful for correcting faults and teaching how to live right.

—2 TIMOTHY 3:16

———✳———

God's word is true, and everything he does is right.

—PSALM 33:4 NCV

———✳———

With all my heart I try to obey you, God. Don't let me break your commands.

—PSALM 119:10

———✳———

Every word of God can be trusted. He protects those who come to him for safety.

—PROVERBS 30:5

———✳———

Your word is like a lamp for my feet and a light for my path.

—PSALM 119:105 NCV

———✳———

Do what God's teaching says; do not just listen and do nothing. When you only sit and listen, you are fooling yourselves.

—JAMES 1:22

———✳———

Only the Lord gives wisdom. Knowledge and understanding come from him.

—PROVERBS 2:6

CHAPTER 7

GOD'S PROMISE FOR YOU

God Will Give You an Inheritance

> Since we are [God's] children, we are his heirs. In fact, together with Christ we are heirs of God's glory.
>
> —ROMANS 8:17 NLT

Have you ever heard the word *heir*? An heir is someone who is given an inheritance, usually by a parent or another family member. Okay . . . but what's an *inheritance*, you ask? Well, an *inheritance* is the stuff an heir gets.

People can inherit all kinds of things, like money or houses, gold or jewels. Perhaps your dad inherited a watch from his granddad, or your mom has a necklace from her great-aunt Ruth.

You are an heir too, and not just in your family here on earth. When you are a child of God, you become an heir of God. And the inheritance your heavenly Father has for you is amazing—a whole jewelry box full of sparkling promises! Best of all, that inheritance can be yours right now. How? By trusting, believing, and following God. Like Joshua did. And just wait until you see how God gave him his inheritance!

After four hundred years of slavery in Egypt, the Israelites were free! God had rescued them, and through Moses, He led them right up to the edge of their inheritance—the promised land. There, God gave His people a promise: "This land is yours. Take it."

All they had to do was trust God's promise.

The Israelites looked at the land. It was rich and good and filled with wonderful things. But it was also filled with mighty cities and powerful warriors who stomped around like giants.

The people forgot all about how God had rescued them. They forgot about the plagues of hopping frogs and buzzing flies. They forgot about the Red Sea splitting open. They even forgot about the manna from heaven and water pouring from rocks.

The Israelites looked at the giants instead of looking at God. They didn't trust God's promise. So He sent them to wander in the wilderness for forty years.

Then Moses died, and Joshua became leader of the Israelites. Their inheritance—the promised land—was still waiting for them. So God gave Joshua the same promise: "This land is yours. Take it."

Joshua looked at the land, at its mighty cities and warriors. Then he looked at God. Joshua trusted God, and so did all the people.

The first city they faced was Jericho. With towering walls all around it, Jericho was impossible to attack. But God had a plan.

"For six days," God said, "take your army and march around the city one time per day. But on the seventh day, march around the city seven times. Have the priests blow their trumpets and tell the people to shout."

Hmm . . . No weapons, no battles. Just marching, trumpeting, and shouting.

But Joshua and the people did exactly as God said. For six days, they marched. Inside Jericho, the people peeped over the walls to watch as thousands and thousands of Israelites paraded around the city. *What kind of attack was this? What were these Israelites up to?*

On the seventh day, the Israelites finished their first lap around the city and kept right on going! Two . . . three . . . four . . . five . . . six times they circled the city. On the seventh lap, the trumpets blasted and the people shouted—and the towering walls of Jericho crumpled to the ground.

Joshua and the Israelites walked straight into the city. God gave them their inheritance, just as He promised He would.

God had a dream for Joshua and the Israelites—and He has a dream for you too. Not just any old dream. It's a dream so big, so great, and so grand that your imagination just isn't big enough to hold it all. Here's the really amazing part: when you choose to become His child, God makes you His heir and gives you an inheritance. Part of that inheritance is everything you need to make His dream for you come true.

Whatever you need, God has it. And He never runs out of anything—not wisdom, not patience, not time or energy or joy. He never waves your prayers away with an, "I'm too tired. Come back tomorrow."

Don't think about what you can or cannot do. Instead, remember what God can do—He can knock down walls with a shout, part rivers and seas, and tell the rain when to fall. So don't worry or be afraid; be bold! Live like you believe God's promise:

You are an heir of God, and He has an inheritance for you!

MY PROMISE TO GOD

I will not worry or be afraid because I am an heir of God—and I know He has an inheritance for me!

Dear God, when I start thinking of what I don't have or can't do, remind me of who I am—Your child and Your heir. You have a dream for me, and I know You'll give me everything I need to make it happen. Amen.

No one has ever seen this. No one has ever heard about it. No one has ever imagined what God has prepared for those who love him.

—I CORINTHIANS 2:9

———✳———

Because we are united with Christ, we have received an inheritance from God.

—EPHESIANS 1:11 NLT

———✳———

I pray that . . . you can understand the confident hope [God] has given to those he called—his holy people who are his rich and glorious inheritance.

—EPHESIANS 1:18 NLT

———✳———

After Moses died, the Lord said to Joshua: "My servant Moses is dead. Now you and all these people go across the Jordan River. Go into the land I am giving to the people of Israel. I promised Moses I would give you this land. So I will give you every place you go in the land."

—JOSHUA 1:1–3

———✳———

"Be strong and brave. Don't be afraid, because the Lord your God will be with you everywhere you go."

—JOSHUA 1:9 NCV

———✳———

Lord, you are great and powerful. You have glory, victory and honor. Everything in heaven and on earth belongs to you. The kingdom belongs to you, Lord. You are the ruler over everything. Riches and honor come from you. You rule everything. You have the power and strength to make anyone great and strong.

—I CHRONICLES 29:11–12

CHAPTER 8

God Is Always with You

The LORD is
with you.

—JUDGES 6:12 NIV

Have you ever been so afraid that you just wanted to hide away from the whole world? Maybe it's from a bully who waits for you after school. Or from a huge test you don't think you can pass. Or from that roomful of people you're too shy to face. Some things are so big and frightening that you don't ever want to face them. It can feel like you're all alone, and you just want to hide.

God understands and gives you a promise: He is with you. *Always.* That doesn't mean you'll never be scared again or never want to hide again. But it does mean you'll never be alone with your fears. That's God's promise to you.

Gideon was a just simple farmer hiding in a hole when God gave him that same promise. If he could just trust God, he'd be able to defeat his fears. But would Gideon choose to trust or to keep hiding?

Gideon was hiding. Huddled in an underground area, he worked quickly to prepare his wheat. Every so often, he peeked over the edge to see if his enemies, the Midianites, were coming.

The Midianites were an army of wandering thieves. They stole the Israelites' crops and destroyed what they couldn't steal. For years, they had bullied Israel. But that was about to change.

"The Lord is with you, mighty warrior!" the angel of the Lord called down to Gideon. "You will save Israel from the Midianites."

Gideon looked up from his hole. "I think you have the wrong person."

But the angel of the Lord knew he did not. "I'll be with you," God promised. Then the angel told Gideon that when he fought the Midianities, it wouldn't be like he was fighting the entire army. "It'll be like you're fighting only one man," he said.

Gideon wanted proof. "Look," he said, "I'll put this wool fleece on the ground. In the morning, if the wool is wet with dew and the ground is dry, I'll believe you." Sure enough, the next morning, the ground was dry while the fleece was dripping wet.

Not wanting to rush into anything, Gideon said, "Let's try it the other way." So, the next morning, the ground was wet and the fleece was dry.

Finally, Gideon was ready to call out the troops. More than thirty-two thousand soldiers gathered to fight. Gideon looked at all those soldiers and started to think, *Okay, we can win this.*

Then God said, "Wait! You have too many men. By the time God finished narrowing down Gideon's army, there were only three hundred soldiers left.

Next God sent Gideon to spy on the Midianites' camp. Gideon overheard two soldiers talking. One said, "I dreamed that a loaf of bread rolled down the hill and flattened one of our tents." The second soldier said, "That means Gideon and his men are going to defeat us!"

Gideon knew there was no way three hundred farmers would defeat the army of Midianites. But he also knew God was with him and his men.

Gideon hurried back to his troops. "Get up!" he said. "God has given the Midianites to you."

Their plan was dangerous and scary. Either God would be with them, or they would be killed. Gideon trusted God's promise to be with him always. He split his men into three groups and surrounded the Midianite camp. Each man carried a trumpet and a jar with a burning torch inside. When Gideon gave the signal, they blew their trumpets and broke the jars. The Midianites panicked and began fighting each other! Gideon and his army won because God was with them.

When the angel of the Lord came to Gideon, the first thing he said was, "The Lord is with you, mighty warrior." *Mighty warrior?* Gideon must have thought. *Do you see me hiding down here in this hole?* The last thing Gideon felt like was a mighty warrior—but that's exactly why the angel called him one. He wanted to remind Gideon that the Lord was on his side, and because of that, he could face anything. Even an army of Midianites.

Chances are, you don't have an enemy army camped in your backyard. But maybe there's something you're afraid to face. And maybe you feel like you have to face it all alone. So let the angel of the Lord remind you too: "God is with you, mighty warrior."

Even though Gideon was weak and his army was small, his God was great. That same great God never leaves your side. No matter how small you may feel, when you step out to face the things that scare you most, God makes you mighty. Trust His promise to Gideon, because it's also His promise to you:

God is with you. Always.

I will not hide from problems. I don't have to be great or mighty. I have all I need. You, God, are with me every moment. When I am afraid, I will call on You.

Dear God, thank You for always being right by my side. Help me trust You and Your strength to take care of me. Amen.

"I am a God who is near," says the Lord.

—JEREMIAH 23:23

——✳——

Even if I walk through a very dark valley, I will not be afraid because you are with me. Your rod and your shepherd's staff comfort me.

—PSALM 23:4

——✳——

"Don't worry, because I am with you. Don't be afraid, because I am your God. I will make you strong and will help you. I will support you with my right hand that saves you."

—ISAIAH 41:10

——✳——

"I am with you and will watch over you wherever you go, and I will bring you back to this land. I will not leave you until I have done what I have promised you."

—GENESIS 28:15 NIV

——✳——

Be strong and brave. Don't be afraid of them. Don't be frightened. The Lord your God will go with you. He will not leave you or forget you.

—DEUTERONOMY 31:6

——✳——

"I am the Lord your God. I am holding your right hand. And I tell you, 'Don't be afraid. I will help you.'"

—ISAIAH 41:13

——✳——

What should we say about this? If God is for us, no one can defeat us.

—ROMANS 8:31 NCV

CHAPTER 9

God Will Rescue His Children

The LORD will
rescue his
servants.

—PSALM 34:22 NIV

Have you ever been stuck in a situation so bad that there was no way you could ever get out on your own? Then, out of nowhere, someone came and saved the day. Maybe it was as simple as someone sitting with you at lunch—rescuing you from eating all alone. Or maybe it was something much bigger, like someone stepping in to help with the family bills when your dad lost his job.

The Bible has another word for those kinds of rescuers: *redeemer*. A redeemer is someone who saves the day. And while it probably isn't a word you hear every day, it's a word you should know. Why? Because Jesus promises to be *your* Redeemer. When you are His child—when you love and serve Him—He saves you.

Through Ruth and Naomi, God shows us the beauty of what a redeemer does. And if anyone ever needed a redeemer, it was Ruth and Naomi.

In the days when the judges ruled, Naomi, her husband, and her two sons left Bethlehem and went to live for a while in the country of Moab. The two sons married Moabite women—Ruth and Orpah. But not long after, Naomi's husband and two sons died.

Naomi was now a widow in a foreign land. She was far from home, heartbroken, and just plain broke. It was time to go home to Bethlehem. The journey would be hard, so Naomi told her daughters-in-law to go back to their own families. Orpah went, but Ruth refused.

"Don't ask me to leave you!" Ruth begged. "Every place you go, I will go. Every place you live, I will live. Your people will be my people. Your God will be my God."

So together, Ruth and Naomi began the long, forty-mile walk back to Bethlehem.

Once they were settled in Naomi's hometown, Ruth went out to the fields to pick up grain the harvest workers left behind. It was hard, hot work. But it was the only way she could get food for Naomi and herself.

The field where Ruth was working belonged to a man named Boaz. He saw Ruth and asked his workers, "Who is that?" When he learned who Ruth was and how she had served Naomi, Boaz decided to help her.

"Stay with my servant girls," he told Ruth. "You'll be safe with them." He gave her bread to eat and water to drink. He even told his workers to drop extra grain for her to pick up and take home.

When evening came, Ruth told Naomi about Boaz and his kindness.

"I know Boaz!" Naomi exclaimed. "He's our relative, so he is one who will take care of us."

And with that, Naomi began to plan. She knew Boaz would sleep on the threshing room floor with his workers. "Go back there," she told Ruth. "Wait until everyone is asleep. Then go and lie down at Boaz's feet." Though it seemed a bit strange, Ruth did exactly as Naomi said.

About midnight, Boaz suddenly woke up—and then sat straight up! A woman was lying at his feet! "Who are you?" he asked.

"It's Ruth. Please spread your blanket over me because you are one who can take care of me."

"Don't worry," Boaz said. Then he set out to be the rescuer—the redeemer—of her dreams. Soon, wedding bells were ringing. Naomi had a home, Boaz had a bride, and the Lord blessed Ruth with a baby. Ruth and Naomi had been redeemed.

71

When Ruth said, "Every place you go, I will go. Every place you live, I will live. Your people will be my people. Your God will be my God," she wasn't just making traveling plans. She was promising to stand by Naomi's side, no matter what happened. She was willing to serve both Naomi and her God.

And it was Ruth's willingness to serve that caught Boaz's attention. Because of it, he was willing to save her, to rescue and redeem her.

When you choose to become a child of God—to love and serve Him—God gives you a whole list of promises. And one of the greatest is this: He will be *your* Redeemer. He will rescue and take care of you. He will save you from your sins. All you have to do is what Ruth did. Put yourself at His feet. Lay down your pride, your worries, your sins, and your selfish ways. Ask your Redeemer to rescue you—to cover you with His blanket of love. He promises that He will. Not for a day, not for a year, but for all time. Because . . .

God will rescue His children.

MY PROMISE TO GOD

I will trust God to be my Redeemer. I know He will rescue me!

Dear God, I lay myself down at Your feet. Please teach me to serve You and to do what is right. And cover me with Your love. Amen.

[God] rescued me because he delights in me.

—PSALM 18:19 NLT

———✳———

This is what the LORD, who saves you, the Holy One of Israel, says: "I am the LORD your God, who teaches you to do what is good, who leads you in the way you should go."

—ISAIAH 48:17 NCV

———✳———

The LORD their God will rescue his people, just as a shepherd rescues his sheep. They will sparkle in his land like jewels in a crown.

—ZECHARIAH 9:16 NLT

———✳———

The Lord is good to those who put their hope in him. He is good to those who look to him for help.

—LAMENTATIONS 3:25

———✳———

The Lord forgives me for all my sins. He heals all my diseases. He saves my life from the grave. He loads me with love and mercy.

—PSALM 103:3–4

———✳———

The LORD defends those who suffer; he defends them in times of trouble. Those who know the LORD trust him, because he will not leave those who come to him.

—PSALM 9:9–10 NCV

———✳———

"Don't be afraid, because I have saved you. I have called you by name, and you are mine."

—ISAIAH 43:1

73

CHAPTER 10

God Will Bring Down Your Giants

The battle is
the LORD's.
—I SAMUEL 17:47 NIV

Some people say there are no such things as giants. Those people are wrong. Giants still roam this world. They are very real and very scary. Real giants are not tall guys who stomp around saying, "Fee-fi-fo-fum!"

Giants sometimes look like that fifth-grade bully who won't leave you alone. Other times they look like a lunchroom full of kids but no one to sit with. Still other times they look like a sickness or sadness. Giants are problems you just don't know how to fix. Giants come in all shapes and sizes. But there's one thing they all have in common: all giants have to be fought.

The question you have to answer is *who* will do the fighting: you or God? David was just a young shepherd boy when he faced that same decision. Would he fight the giant Goliath on his own? Or would he allow God to fight for him? His answer to that question made all the difference.

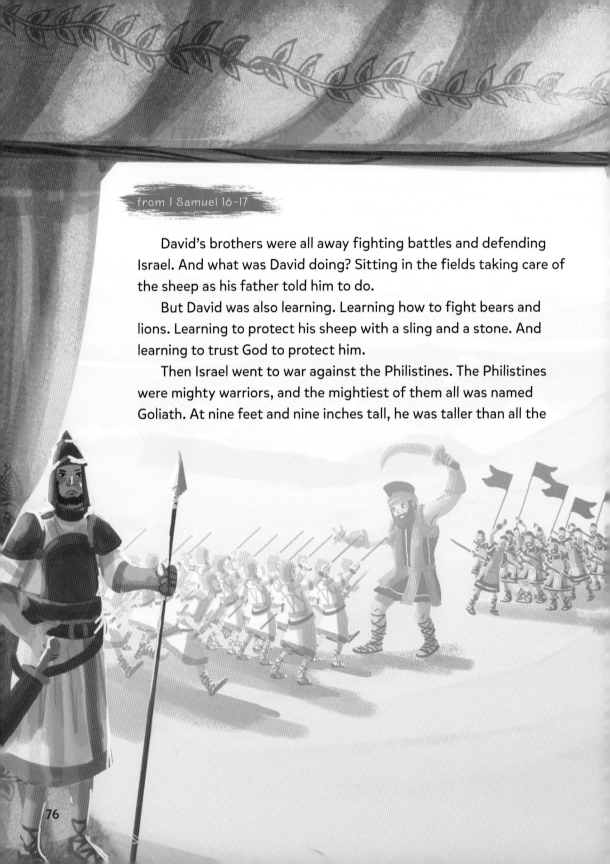

from 1 Samuel 16–17

David's brothers were all away fighting battles and defending Israel. And what was David doing? Sitting in the fields taking care of the sheep as his father told him to do.

But David was also learning. Learning how to fight bears and lions. Learning to protect his sheep with a sling and a stone. And learning to trust God to protect him.

Then Israel went to war against the Philistines. The Philistines were mighty warriors, and the mightiest of them all was named Goliath. At nine feet and nine inches tall, he was taller than all the

Israelites. He wore 160 pounds of armor, and his shield was so big that another man was ordered to carry it. Twice every day he marched out to the front of the battlefield and double-dog dared the Israelites to fight him.

But no one would. Goliath woke the Israelites each morning with his dares and sent them scurrying into their tents at night with his insults and jeers. Twice a day for forty days he insulted both the Israelites and their God. The men in Israel's army were too afraid to fight Goliath.

Then scrawny, young David showed up. His father had sent him with food for his brothers. He'd only been in the Israelites' camp a little while when Goliath marched out to repeat his daily challenge. David listened and waited for someone to charge the giant. Surely someone would stop this giant, but no one did. He looked around. No one was going to go. David couldn't believe it.

Furious, he asked, "Who does this rotten Philistine think he is? Does he really think he can speak against the armies of God?"

But David's brothers were angry with him. "Who do you think *you* are? Go home and take care of your sheep!" they told him.

But David refused. He went to King Saul and asked if he could fight Goliath for the Israelites. King Saul agreed and even offered David his own armor to wear. But David refused, saying, "The Lord who saved me from the lion and the bear will also save me from this giant."

David marched out to meet Goliath, stopping only to scoop five smooth stones from a stream. He slipped them into his pouch. He carried his stick in one hand and kept his sling ready in the other.

At the same time, Goliath marched toward David. When Goliath saw that David was only a boy, he was disgusted. "Do you think I'm a dog that you come at me with a stick?"

David shouted back, "You come at me with a sword and a spear. But I am coming in the name of the Lord of heaven's armies! Today, He will give you to me. The battle belongs to Him!"

Goliath raised his sword. David, the shepherd, slipped a stone in his sling and slung it. The stone hit that hard-headed Goliath with a crack, and Goliath went down.

David defeated the giant with only a sling and a stone. But David knew the truth. He didn't really defeat Goliath; the Lord did. God fought for him.

Goliath had only one goal: to scare the Israelites until they didn't even dare to fight. Your Enemy—that devilish Devil—wants to do the same to you. And he uses all kinds of giants to do it.

Some things feel like a battle. And they can be scary. But you have to remember *whose* battle it is. You have what David had—a God who will fight for you. You do not march into battle alone. You do not struggle alone. You do not face your giants alone. Because God is always with you.

And God does more than just promise to be with you. He gives you another, even more amazing promise: He will fight for you. That promise wasn't just for David and his giant. It's for you and those things that scare you too. So next time you hear some giant snort and snarl, threaten and terrorize, remind yourself and him that . . .

This battle belongs to the Lord.

MY PROMISE TO GOD

I will not worry. I will be brave and trust God to fight the giant problems for me.

*

Dear God, when I have to face something big and scary and it feels like a giant problem, help me remember that You will fight for me. Amen.

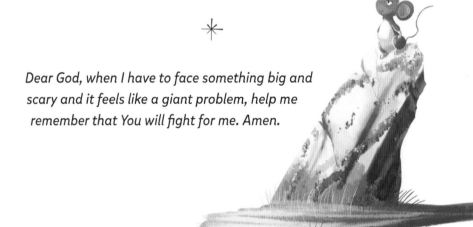

Our God will fight for us.

—NEHEMIAH 4:20

———✳———

[Jesus said,] "Satan has asked to test all of you as a farmer tests his wheat. Simon, Simon, I have prayed that you will not lose your faith! Help your brothers be stronger when you come back to me."

—LUKE 22:31-32

———✳———

Elisha said, "Don't be afraid. The army that fights for us
is larger than the one against us." Then Elisha prayed,
"Lord, open my servant's eyes. Let him see."
The Lord opened the eyes of the young man. And he saw that the mountain was full of horses and chariots of fire all around Elisha.

—2 KINGS 6:16-17

———✳———

[David said,] "The Lord saved me from a lion and a bear.
He will also save me from this Philistine."
Saul said to David, "Go, and may the Lord be with you."

—1 SAMUEL 17:37

———✳———

In all these things we are completely victorious
through God who showed his love for us.

—ROMANS 8:37 NCV

———✳———

"You will not succeed by your own strength or by your own power. The power will come from my Spirit," says the Lord of heaven's armies.

—ZECHARIAH 4:6

CHAPTER 11

God Will Hear Your Prayers

> When a believing person prays, great things happen.
>
> —JAMES 5:16 NCV

When you have a problem, who do you turn to for help? Chances are, you have lots of people you can go to. Parents, grandparents, teachers, preachers, and friends. But Someone else is waiting to help you too. Someone who's always ready to listen. It's God. And when you talk to Him, great things happen.

Just ask Elijah. He was a prophet who lived eight hundred years before Jesus was born. His land had one evil king after another. And the one who was now ruling—Ahab—was the most evil of them all. But perhaps the worst thing was that the people didn't seem to care.

Then Elijah came blazing onto the scene, and he was ready to really set some things on fire. But he didn't start that fire with a match. He started with a prayer. And then Elijah trusted God to do the rest.

For three years, there had been no rain. Not a drop. Not a drip.

Because Elijah had prayed and asked God to stop the rain. So God did. For three years.

Elijah was trying to get the wicked King Ahab's attention. To get the Israelite people's attention. He wanted them to remember that only God was God. But they didn't. They kept bowing down to their phony god, Baal.

One day, God told Elijah to go to King Ahab and give it one more try.

"Let's decide this once and for all," Elijah told Ahab. "Tell the people to meet me at Mount Carmel. Bring the 450 prophets of your false god, Baal. We'll see who the true God is."

At Mount Carmel, Elijah challenged the people: "Decide who you will serve—God or Baal!"

But the people wouldn't answer. So Elijah told the 450 prophets of Baal: "You get a sacrifice, and I'll get a sacrifice. You build an altar, and I'll build an altar. You ask your god to send fire, and I'll ask my God to send fire. The God who answers by fire is the true God. I'll even let you go first."

From morning to noon, the prophets of Baal prayed to their god. But there was no answer. They danced round and round the altar. Still no answer.

Elijah began to make fun of them. "Shout louder! Maybe Baal is thinking or traveling. Maybe he's in the bathroom!" Elijah snickered. "Or maybe he's sleeping—shout louder so he'll wake up!"

The prophets prayed louder and danced wilder. They even cut themselves with swords and spears to try to get Baal's attention. Nothing worked. Baal still did not answer.

Evening came, and Elijah asked for his turn. He built an altar and dug a ditch around it. He piled the wood and the sacrifice on top. Then he had twelve jugs of water poured over the altar! The water ran off the top, down the sides, and filled up the ditch.

Then Elijah prayed: "Oh God, show these people that You are Lord. Answer my prayer."

God answered in a flash! Fire shot down from heaven. It burned up the sacrifice, the wood, the stones, the dust, and even the water. The people fell to the ground and cried out, "The Lord is God! The Lord is God!"

God showed His great power when Elijah prayed. Because Elijah trusted God to keep His promise: *Pray to Me, and I will answer you.*

Elijah prayed, and God listened. Elijah believed God would answer his prayer, and God did. Because that's what God promises: He will listen, and He will answer.

You don't have to be some sort of prayer superstar either. Just believe God will do what He says He will do. Elijah himself was just an ordinary man. He had doubts, he had questions, and he had fears. But when he prayed, he believed God would answer. And—*POW!*—the soaking-wet altar exploded into a great blazing fire.

God loves hearing your prayers too. Why? Your prayers matter to God because *you* matter to God. After all, you aren't just anybody. You are *His* child. He loves you, and He loves listening to you. He never says, "Come back later." He's always ready to listen.

Does that mean God will do exactly what you ask? Maybe. Sometimes He tells you no or not now. Or maybe He'll do even more than you imagine. Trust God to know what's best for you. And trust His promise to answer, because . . .

When a believing person prays, great things happen.

MY PROMISE TO GOD

I promise to pray. I promise to believe that God will answer and trust that His answers are best for me.

Dear God, You are the Lord of everything, but You still want to hear from me. That is amazing! Thank You for listening to me when I pray. Help me trust You, no matter how You answer me.

"Pray to me, and I will answer you."

—JEREMIAH 33:3

The Lord is close to everyone who prays to him, to all who truly pray to him.

—PSALM 145:18

"You will call my name. You will come to me and pray to me.
And I will listen to you. You will search for me. And when you
search for me with all your heart, you will find me!"

—JEREMIAH 29:12-13

Don't worry about anything; instead, pray about everything. Tell
God what you need, and thank him for all he has done.

—PHILIPPIANS 4:6 NLT

Let us, then, feel free to come before God's throne. Here there is grace.
And we can receive mercy and grace to help us when we need it.

—HEBREWS 4:16

"Keep on asking, and you will receive what you ask for. Keep on seeking,
and you will find. Keep on knocking, and the door will be opened to you."

—MATTHEW 7:7 NLT

"If two or three people come together in my name, I am there with them."

—MATTHEW 18:20

CHAPTER 12

God Will Make It All End Well

In everything God
works for the
good of those
who love him.

—ROMANS 8:28

Are there times when you *know* what you should do, but you just don't want to do it? Times when it's easier to do nothing at all? Perhaps you need to tell your friend something that she isn't going to like. It would be easier to say nothing. Or perhaps you need to stand up for someone who can't stand up for himself. But that might make you a target. It would be easier to do nothing.

When you have to choose between doing what's right and doing nothing at all, it's tempting to take the easy way out. *Don't.* Because God has a promise for you: If you will do what's right, then He'll make it all end well.

Queen Esther knew the right thing to do. But doing it would put her own life in danger. Would she take the easy way out? Or would she trust God to make everything end well?

Queen Esther paced back and forth across her room in the palace. She had a decision to make, and it was a matter of life and death.

Her people, the Jews, were in danger. Her uncle, Mordecai, wanted her to go to her husband to try to save them. After all, her husband, King Xerxes, ruled all of Persia. But it wasn't that simple. The king didn't know Esther was a Jew. And many people in Persia hated the Jews.

In fact, it was Haman—the king's evil advisor—who had put her in danger. He *hated* the Jews. And because Esther's uncle, Mordecai, wouldn't bow down to him, Haman hated Mordecai most of all.

So Haman convinced the king that the Jews were a threat to his kingdom. The king then signed a law that said, on this one particular day, any Persian could kill any Jew. *And* he could take everything the Jew owned. That day was coming soon.

Which was why Mordecai wanted Esther to go to the king. The problem was that no one—not even the queen—could go to the king without being called. And it had been thirty days since Xerxes had called for Esther. If she went to see the king without being called, she could be killed.

Esther stopped pacing and shook her head. She couldn't do it. It was too dangerous. She sent a message to her uncle with the news.

Mordecai couldn't take no for an answer. Too many lives were in danger. "Just because you live in the palace," he said, "doesn't mean you'll be safe.

You might keep quiet, and someone else will save the Jews. Who knows? Maybe you were chosen queen just for this moment."

Esther knew her uncle was right. She had to go to the king. She sent another message: "Gather all the Jews. Don't eat or drink for three days. I and my servant girls will also give up eating. Then I'll go to the king. If I die, I die."

Mordecai did everything Esther told him to do.

Three days later Esther stood outside the king's throne room. She took a deep breath, straightened her shoulders, and walked inside.

The king saw her . . . and smiled. "What is it, Queen Esther? What do you want to ask me? I will give you as much as half of my kingdom."

It was Esther's turn to smile. God was using her to save her people. And everything would end all right.

Esther's real decision wasn't about going to the king. It wasn't about whether or not to put herself in danger. Her real decision was about whether or not to trust God. Esther decided to do what was right and trust that God would make sure everything ended all right.

That's a promise God makes to His people. He doesn't say the right choice will be the easy one. And He doesn't promise that bad things will never happen. But He does promise that when you love Him and choose to follow Him, He will use everything for your good.

Your life is a bit like a puzzle. There are beautiful pieces and ugly pieces and ordinary pieces. When you look at just one of those pieces by itself—especially an ugly one—it's hard to see how it can be used for good. But God promises to use *all* the pieces of your life—yes, even the ugly ones—to create a beautiful masterpiece.

Do what's right, and God will make it all end well.

MY PROMISE TO GOD

I will do what is right and trust God to make things work for good.

Dear God, please give me the courage and the strength to do what is right. I will trust You to make it all end well. Amen.

Do what God's teaching says; do not just listen and do nothing.

—JAMES 1:22

———✳———

If you pay attention to the commands of the LORD your
God that I give you this day and carefully follow them, you
will always be at the top, never at the bottom.

—DEUTERONOMY 28:13 NIV

———✳———

The LORD will work out his plans for my life—for
your faithful love, O LORD, endures forever.

—PSALM 138:8 NLT

———✳———

I cry out to God Most High, to God who will fulfill his purpose for me.

—PSALM 57:2 NLT

———✳———

God began doing a good work in you. And he will continue it
until it is finished when Jesus Christ comes again.

—PHILIPPIANS 1:6

———✳———

Everything you say and everything you do should
all be done for Jesus your Lord.

—COLOSSIANS 3:17

———✳———

God blesses those who patiently endure testing and
temptation. Afterward they will receive the crown of life
that God has promised to those who love him.

—JAMES 1:12 NLT

CHAPTER 13

God Will Give Grace to the Humble

God is against
the proud, but
he gives grace
to the humble.

—I PETER 5:5

Have you ever been proud of something you've done? Maybe you won an award for a picture you drew, got first place in the race, or aced a test. It's okay to be proud of what you do, but don't be so proud of yourself that you think you are better than others!

Don't forget God—He's the One who makes you able to do everything you do. That picture was drawn with talents He gave you. The race was won with legs He created. And you wouldn't have aced that test without the mind He made.

God wants you to remember that every good thing you have is a gift from Him (James 1:17). That's called being *humble*. A humble person is quick to admit the need for God, glad to confess sin, willing to put God first.

King Nebuchadnezzar was *not* humble. And he learned that when you forget to be humble, God will remind you—the hard way!

King Nebuchadnezzar was a mighty man—and he knew it. No one's palace was bigger. No one's army was stronger. No one's treasures were richer.

To show how awesome he was, he built a ninety-foot tall golden statue and told everyone to bow down to it. Three young Hebrews—Shadrach, Meshach, and Abednego—said no. They would only bow down to God. So the king fired up the furnace and had the young men thrown in. When they stepped out of the flames—not even smelling like smoke—Nebuchadnezzar was amazed by their God.

But the king still thought he, Nebuchadnezzar, was even more amazing.

Twenty or thirty years passed, and everything was going great for Nebuchadnezzar. Until he had a dream. Because none of his own fortune-tellers could explain it, he called for Daniel.

"I dreamed there was a great tree," Nebuchadnezzar told Daniel. "It was so tall it touched the sky. Wild animals found shelter under it, and birds lived in its branches. But an angel came and cut the tree down. Only a stump was left. Then the angel said, 'Let the man live with the animals. Let him think and act like an animal for seven years.'

"What does this dream mean?" the king asked.

Daniel gulped. This was not a good dream. "My king," he said, "*you* are that tree! You'll become like an animal, and you'll live with the animals for seven years. The stump means that you'll get your kingdom back when you learn that God is Ruler over all. So, my king, please humble yourself before it is too late."

God gave Nebuchadnezzar a whole year to change his proud ways. But he didn't.

One day, as the king was out walking, he said, "Just look at this great city. *I* built it by *my* power to show how great *I* am."

The words were barely out of his mouth when a voice called down from heaven: "King Nebuchadnezzar, your royal power has been taken away from you."

Nebuchadnezzar's hair grew long like the feathers of an eagle. His nails became like the claws of a bird. The people forced him away, and he began eating grass like an ox.

Seven years passed
before Nebuchadnezzar
could think like a man again.
Then he looked up to heaven and praised
God as Ruler of all. Because the king had at last
learned to be humble, God gave him back his kingdom.
God gave him grace.

God sent Nebuchadnezzar three messages warning him not to be so proud. The first message was the fiery furnace. It showed him that God is even greater than fire. The second message was the dream—it meant that even though he might be a big tree today, tomorrow he can be just an ugly stump. And then there was Daniel's warning: humble yourself before it is too late. But Nebuchadnezzar didn't humble himself, so God did it for him.

Over and over, the Bible tells us that God hates pride. He hates it when we think we can do everything on our own. Why? Because God wants to bless us. And only when we admit we need Him can He give us His greatest blessing of all: *grace*. Grace washes away our sins and welcomes us into heaven. God gives grace to the humble because the humble know they need His grace.

Remember God, and praise Him for all He does for you. Because . . . When you humble yourself before God, He blesses you.

MY PROMISE TO GOD

I will not think more highly of myself than I should. I will put God first!

Dear God, please forgive me for the times that I forget to praise You and thank You. No one is greater than You. Amen.

Though the LORD is great, he cares for the humble,
but he keeps his distance from the proud.

—PSALM 138:6 NLT

———✳———

"I give new life to those who are humble."

—ISAIAH 57:15

———✳———

"God blesses those who are humble, for they
will inherit the whole earth."

—MATTHEW 5:5 NLT

———✳———

He guides the humble in what is right and teaches them his way.

—PSALM 25:9 NIV

———✳———

The LORD is pleased with his people; he saves the humble.

—PSALM 149:4 NCV

———✳———

"Accept my work and learn from me. I am gentle and
humble in spirit. And you will find rest for your souls."

—MATTHEW 11:29

———✳———

Whatever is good and perfect is a gift coming down to us from
God our Father, who created all the lights in the heavens.

—JAMES 1:17 NLT

CHAPTER 14

GOD'S PROMISE FOR YOU

God Will Work in You

God is
working
in you.

—PHILIPPIANS 2:13

Have you ever felt like you weren't *enough*? Not old enough to help. Not tall enough to ride the roller coaster. Not good enough to make the team. Just not *enough*.

Maybe you've even felt that way when it comes to God—not good enough. You don't see how you can possibly do all those things the Bible says you should do.

If you've ever felt that way, God has a promise for you: you don't have to be good enough, and you don't have to do anything on your own, because God is working in you. When you choose to follow Him, God's Spirit comes to live and work inside you—He makes the impossible possible. God changes your "can't" into "can" and your "not good enough" into "more than enough."

Believe God, trust His promises, and follow Him. That's what Mary did . . . and you can too.

Mary's day began like any other.

She woke with the sun and helped with breakfast and chores. She washed and cleaned, gathered and baked. She thought about Joseph, the man she was going to marry. And she wondered what it would be like to have her own home and family.

It was just another ordinary day.

Until the angel came.

Mary had just stepped out into the small garden behind her home. It was quiet and peaceful, and she was alone. But not for long.

An angel suddenly appeared before her. His name was Gabriel, and God had sent him with a message for Mary.

"Greetings!" Gabriel said. "The Lord has blessed you, and He is with you."

Mary wasn't sure what to think about this. After all, it's not every day that an angel pops into your backyard. "What does this mean?" she asked.

"Don't be afraid, Mary," the angel smiled. "God is pleased with you. You are going to have a Son, and you'll name Him Jesus. The people will call Him the Son of the Most High. God will give Him the throne of King David. He will rule over the people of Israel forever. And His kingdom will never end."

Mary blinked. *A baby?* "How can this be possible?" she asked. "I'm not even married!"

"The Holy Spirit will come upon you," the angel told her. "The baby will be the holy Son of God. Remember your cousin Elizabeth?"

Mary nodded. Elizabeth had never been able to have a child—a fact that made her very sad. And now that she was growing old, everyone thought it was too late.

"No one believed she'd ever have a baby," the angel said. "But she has been pregnant for six months now. Everything is possible for God!"

Mary shook her head in amazement. This was all so hard to believe. But there was one thing she knew for certain: this angel had been sent from God. All her life, Mary had trusted her Lord. Even though this news was confusing—and more than a little frightening—she would trust Him to take care of her now.

She looked up at the angel and said, "I am God's servant. Let this happen to me just as you say!"

Mary chose to believe the wildest of promises—that Christ would live in her. And because she believed, Christ can also live in you.

Mary could have given the angel Gabriel a thousand different excuses. *I'm too poor. Too simple. Too ordinary.* She could have said, "Thanks, but this really isn't a good time for me. I've already made other plans for my life." But she didn't. Instead, she welcomed God into her life. And because she did, you can too.

God makes you the same offer He gave Mary—for His Spirit to come and to live and work in you. Just take a look at the big message inside that little word *in*. God isn't just *for* you or *with* you. He isn't standing close by. When you are His child, His Spirit lives *in* you. And once He's in, He gets to work.

That doesn't mean you get to sit back and do nothing. Like Mary, you have to cooperate with God. How? Pray. Read His Word. And instead of telling God what you want, ask, "What can I do for You?"

It's your choice: Will you make excuses? Will you say, "Thanks, but I've made other plans"? Or will you welcome God into your life? Trust His promise, and . . .

God will work in you.

"I will put a new way of thinking inside you. I will take out the stubborn hearts of stone from your bodies, and I will give you obedient hearts of flesh. I will put my Spirit inside you and help you live by my rules and carefully obey my laws."

—EZEKIEL 36:26–27 NCV

———✳———

Christ will make his home in your hearts as you trust in him. Your roots will grow down into God's love and keep you strong.

—EPHESIANS 3:17 NLT

———✳———

"Before I made you in your mother's womb. I chose you. Before you were born, I set you apart for a special work."

—JEREMIAH 1:5

———✳———

God decided to let his people know this rich and glorious truth which he has for all people. This truth is Christ himself, who is in you. He is our only hope for glory.

—COLOSSIANS 1:27

———✳———

The person who obeys God's commands lives in God. And God lives in him.

—1 JOHN 3:24

———✳———

"Here I am! I stand at the door and knock. If anyone hears my voice and opens the door, I will come in and eat with him. And he will eat with me."

—REVELATION 3:20

———✳———

To do this, I work and struggle, using Christ's great strength that works so powerfully in me.

—COLOSSIANS 1:29

CHAPTER 15

Jesus Understands You

Our high priest is able
to understand our
weaknesses. He was
tempted in every way that
we are, but he did not sin.

—HEBREWS 4:15

Have you ever thought, *It would be so easy to lie?* Just one little fib, and you'd be out of trouble. Or maybe you've been tempted to do a quick snatch when no one's looking—and that thing you want would be yours. You know it's wrong. You know you shouldn't. But it's just so tempting.

Believe it or not, Jesus understands. He understands every temptation you'll ever face. How? Because He faced them too. That's part of why He came to earth—to live and to grow up just the way you do. He understands everything you will go through.

The Son of God started His life on earth as a tiny baby. Just like you. With His birth in that Bethlehem stable, God gave His people a promise: Whatever you're facing, whatever you're struggling with, whatever is tempting you, God understands. He's been there. And because He's been there, God gets you.

The streets were dusty and crowded. Joseph gently pushed his way past the people, leading the donkey behind him.

He stopped at the small inn and knocked. Laughter floated out through the window, but no one came to the door. Joseph knocked louder. The door swung open. Before Joseph could even ask, the innkeeper said, "No room, no room!" And he began to close the door.

"Wait!" Joseph lifted a hand toward Mary, who sat atop the donkey. "My wife is going to have a baby. Please, is there somewhere we could stay? Anywhere will do."

The innkeeper was not unkind. But his inn was full. Still, he looked at Mary. "The stables are just over there," he pointed. "They aren't much, but they're warm and dry."

"Thank you," Joseph said. He looked back at Mary, and she nodded. Then he led the donkey toward the stables.

Inside, Joseph laid a blanket over a pile of hay and helped Mary settle on it. In that small stable—with the sounds and smells of animals all around her—Mary had her baby. They named Him Jesus, just as the angel told them to do.

Mary and Joseph smiled down at the wonder of Him. This baby who was the Son of God. They touched His tiny nose and counted His ten tiny fingers and ten tiny toes. Mary wrapped Him in some clothes, warm and snug. As Jesus drifted off to sleep, she gently laid Him in a manger. The Son of God slept in the animals' feeding box.

Suddenly, shepherds swept into the stable with an incredible story to tell. Seeing the mother and sleeping child, they shushed and tiptoed over to peek at the Savior.

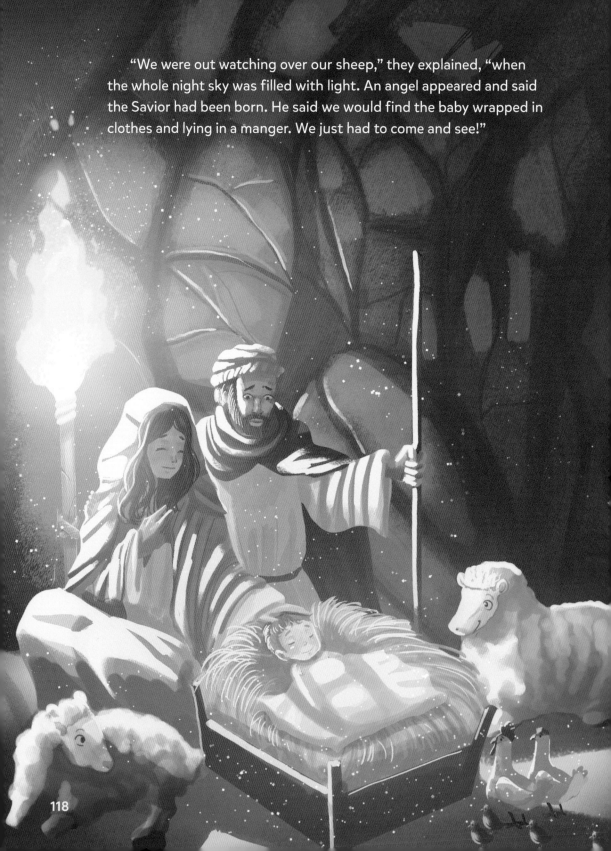

"We were out watching over our sheep," they explained, "when the whole night sky was filled with light. An angel appeared and said the Savior had been born. He said we would find the baby wrapped in clothes and lying in a manger. We just had to come and see!"

After a few more *oohs* and *aahs*, the shepherds went back to their sheep, praising God for all they had seen and heard.

As Mary lifted Jesus into her arms, she thought about everything that had happened and treasured those things in her heart.

This Child—this Son of God—would live and learn and grow up just like His people did. He would understand. And because He understood, He could show His people the way.

Jesus could have come to earth any way He wanted. He could have chosen to be rich and powerful. He could've chosen not to come at all. But He did come. As a tiny baby. So He could live life just like you.

Jesus was once just your age. He skinned His knees, and His brothers and sisters probably got on His nerves. There were chores He didn't like to do. Jesus wept when He lost a friend, and He hurt when a friend betrayed Him. He got hungry in the wilderness and once got so tired that He slept through a storm. Because of all this, Jesus can promise that He understands.

Why is this promise important? Because if you ever wonder if Jesus knows what it's like to be you, He does. If you ever wonder whether God listens, He does. If you ever wonder if the God of all the heavens could— in a million years—understand what it's like to be bullied or hurt or lied about or tempted to sin, He does.

Jesus understands you.

MY PROMISE TO GOD

I will tell Jesus everything, because He understands me.

Dear Jesus, sometimes it feels like no one understands.
But I know You do because You were once like me.
Help me, now, to be more like You. Amen.

The Lord said to me, "My grace is enough for you. When you are weak, then my power is made perfect in you." So I am very happy to brag about my weaknesses. Then Christ's power can live in me.

—2 CORINTHIANS 12:9

———✳———

The Lord is faithful. He will give you strength and protect you from the Evil One.

—2 THESSALONIANS 3:3

———✳———

The Lord hears good people when they cry out to him. He saves them from all their troubles.

—PSALM 34:17

———✳———

The Word became a man and lived among us. We saw his glory—the glory that belongs to the only Son of the Father. The Word was full of grace and truth.

—JOHN 1:14

———✳———

No one has seen God, but Jesus is exactly like him.

—COLOSSIANS 1:15

———✳———

Because [Jesus] himself suffered when he was tempted. he is able to help those who are being tempted.

—HEBREWS 2:18 NIV

———✳———

"I am the good shepherd. I know my sheep, and my sheep know me, just as the Father knows me, and I know the Father. I give my life for the sheep."

—JOHN 10:14–15

CHAPTER 16

GOD'S PROMISE FOR YOU

God Will Grow His Kingdom in Your Heart

"God's kingdom is within you."

—LUKE 17:21

When you hear the word *kingdom*, what do you think of? Maybe you think of fairy-tale kingdoms with their knights and battles, their ruling kings and castles full of riches. Or perhaps you think of powerful kingdoms here on earth that rule over all their people. At least, that's what people usually think of.

So when the prophets of the Old Testament promised over and over again that the kingdom of God was coming, the Jews watched and waited for a kingdom of great power and might. A kingdom that would rescue them and rule the whole world.

But God's idea of His kingdom was very different. It had a lot less to do with power and castles and riches, and a whole lot more to do with changing hearts and minds.

The last thing the Jewish people expected was for the kingdom of God to be built not with weapons but with faith and love in the hearts of God's people. And they certainly didn't expect His kingdom to begin with a poor carpenter born in a stable and named Jesus.

from Mark 4:1–20

Jesus sat down near the lake to teach. But so many people gathered around that He stood up and got into a boat. He went a little ways out on the water, so the waves would carry His voice for everyone to hear.

Then He began to tell a story about a farmer.

"A farmer went out to plant his seed," Jesus said. "As he walked along, he scattered handfuls in front of him.

"Some seed fell on the hard path, and birds snatched it up. Some seed fell on the rocks and sprouted up fast. But it didn't have deep roots. When the hot sun shone down, those plants died. Other seed fell in with the thorny weeds. The weeds grew up and choked out the good plants so that they didn't make any grain.

"But some seed," Jesus said with a smile, "some seed fell in the good, rich dirt. Those seeds grew and grew and made a good crop of grain. Some of the plants made thirty times more grain. Others made sixty or even a hundred times more grain."

"Do you understand My story?" Jesus asked.

The disciples looked at each other and then back at Jesus. They shook their heads. They loved to hear Jesus' stories, but they weren't always great at figuring out what those stories meant.

Jesus explained, "The farmer is the person who shares God's Word with other people. The soil is like the people's hearts.

"Sometimes the Word is like the seed that falls on the hard path. That is, some people hear God's Word, but their hearts are hard and the Devil quickly snatches it away.

"Other people hear God's Word and believe it with joy. But as soon as trouble comes, they give up and stop believing. They're like the seed that fell on the rocks.

"Still others hear and believe, but worry, greed, and the things of this world choke out their belief so it stops growing. They're like the seed that fell into the thorny weeds.

"But others are like the seed that fell on the good, rich dirt. They hear and believe. They love and trust God. They share His Word so more and more people come to believe—sometimes thirty more, sometimes sixty or even a hundred times more."

This is how the kingdom of God comes into the world—like a farmer sowing his seed. It grows inside the hearts of those who hear. Who love and trust and believe.

When Jesus began His ministry on earth, it wasn't anything like what the people expected. He didn't come with a crown to conquer the world. His kingdom isn't about armies or weapons or war. And His kingdom isn't just for heaven; it's already here. It's in the hearts of His people. Hearts willing to love and believe. Hearts that are good soil for the seed of His Word.

But what if your heart isn't good soil right now? What if it's filled with weeds of worry? That's when it's time to talk to Jesus. He already knows about all those things that worry you. The troubles, the friends, that big test on Monday. And His answer is simple: "Don't worry."

Just look at how He clothes the flowers and takes care of the birds. He'll do so much more for you! Seek His kingdom and what He wants first. And He'll take care of everything that worries you (Matthew 6:33).

God's kingdom is so much greater than any kingdom of earth—and His kingdom is for you. Because when you believe, He gives you this amazing promise:

God will grow His kingdom right within your heart.

MY PROMISE TO GOD

God's kingdom is so much greater than I could ever imagine— and I will trust Him to grow His kingdom in my own heart.

Dear God, please soften my heart so Your Word will grow deep inside me. And help me share Your Word and Your kingdom with everyone I meet. Amen.

Jesus said, "My kingdom does not belong to this world."

—JOHN 18:36

———✳———

In the kingdom of God, eating and drinking are not important. The important things are living right with God, peace, and joy in the Holy Spirit.

—ROMANS 14:17 NCV

———✳———

The Lord has set his throne in heaven. And his kingdom rules over everything.

—PSALM 103:19

———✳———

This is what the Lord says: "I am the Lord. There is no other God."

—ISAIAH 45:18

———✳———

Create in me a pure heart, God. Make my spirit right again.

—PSALM 51:10

———✳———

"Seek first God's kingdom and what God wants. Then all your other needs will be met as well."

—MATTHEW 6:33 NCV

CHAPTER 17

Jesus Will Pray for You

Jesus . . . is sitting
in the place of honor
at God's right hand,
pleading for us.

—ROMANS 8:34 NLT

Has someone ever stood up for you? Or has someone stepped in and saved your day? Maybe it was as simple as someone picking you to be on his team when you thought no one would. Or someone sitting with you at lunch when you were the new kid at school. It's a pretty wonderful thing to know that you aren't on your own.

The fact is, you're never on your own. Jesus is standing up for you and praying for you; that's His promise. Whenever trouble starts heading your way, Jesus heads for His heavenly Father and asks Him to bless and protect you. When you forget to pray, He remembers. When you are full of fears, Jesus is full of faith. But don't think that Jesus prays for you only when times are tough. No! He is *always* praying for you—every moment of every day.

Even so, when you're in the middle of a storm of trouble, that's when it's most tempting to ask, "Where's Jesus?" That's what His disciples did. And the answer for them is the same as the answer for you.

from Matthew 14:22-33

The disciples watched Jesus wave good-bye to the people.

It had been a long day. More than five thousand people had crowded around Jesus on the shores of Lake Galilee. He had taught them and miraculously fed them. Now, He sent the people back to their homes and His disciples to their boat.

"Sail to the other side of the lake," He told them. "I'll meet you there."

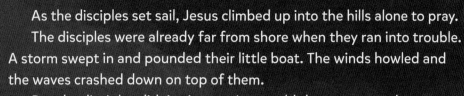

As the disciples set sail, Jesus climbed up into the hills alone to pray.

The disciples were already far from shore when they ran into trouble. A storm swept in and pounded their little boat. The winds howled and the waves crashed down on top of them.

But the disciples didn't give up. Jesus told them to go to the other side of the lake, so that's where they were heading. They dug their paddles into the raging sea, inching forward only to be pushed back again. It was a losing battle, and they knew it. Their faces were splattered with rain and fear.

And where was Jesus? He was up in the hills, praying. He didn't eat. He didn't sleep. He'd served all day, and now He was praying all night. Even in the storm. Or maybe He prayed *because* there was a storm. The rain soaked His robe, and the wind ripped at His hair and stung His face. Still He prayed.

After a time, Jesus got up and began His journey to the other side of the lake. Rather than walk all the way around it, Jesus decided to walk straight across. He was the Son of God, after all.

It was dark, and the disciples were exhausted but still battling the storm. Squinting through the rain and darkness, they saw something. No . . . Someone! Someone was walking toward them *on the water*!

"It's a ghost!" they shouted. They were terrified.

"Don't be afraid," Jesus called out to them. "It is I!"

"If that's really You, Lord," Peter said, "then tell me to come to You on the water."

"Come."

Peter stepped out of the boat and onto the water. He was doing it! He was walking on the water! But then he looked at the waves and felt the wind—and Peter began to sink. "Lord, save me!" he cried.

Jesus reached down and caught Peter. As they stepped into the boat, the storm stopped. Awed and amazed, the disciples said, "Truly You are the Son of God!"

Jesus knew His disciples were caught in a terrible storm. So He prayed—and then He came to save them.

You might think that Jesus would have been shielded from the storms. After all, He's the Son of God. He shouldn't get wet or cold or blown around by the wind! You might also think that since you're a child of God, you should be shielded from the storms of life too. Right? Wrong!

The truth of the matter is that this life comes with storms. Jesus even tells us, "In this world you will have trouble" (John 16:33). Sometimes we create our own storms. We tell a lie, take what isn't ours, or hang out with the wrong crowd. Other times, the storm just happens. It might be stormy weather, like the disciples faced in their boat. Or it might be a test you really studied for but still flunked. A race you trained for but still lost. A friend you loved who still moved away.

Storms will come. Even when you do everything right. But when they do, Jesus promises to do for you what He did for His first disciples:

Jesus will pray for you—and then He will come to help you.

Dear Jesus, it's hard to imagine that You actually pray for me. But I'm so very glad that You do! Amen.

[Jesus] is able always to save those who come to God through him because he always lives, asking God to help them.

—HEBREWS 7:25 NCV

———✳———

[Jesus] went into heaven itself. He is there now before God to help us.

—HEBREWS 9:24

———✳———

If anyone does sin, we have Jesus Christ to help us. He is the Righteous One. He defends us before God the Father.

—1 JOHN 2:1

———✳———

"The Son of Man did not come for other people to serve him. He came to serve others. The Son of Man came to give his life to save many people."

—MATTHEW 20:28

———✳———

We do not know how to pray as we should. But the Spirit himself speaks to God for us, even begs God for us. The Spirit speaks to God with deep feelings that words cannot explain.

—ROMANS 8:26

———✳———

"I have prayed that you will not lose your faith!"

—LUKE 22:32

———✳———

Early the next morning, Jesus woke and left the house while it was still dark. He went to a place to be alone and pray.

—MARK 1:35

CHAPTER 18

Jesus Will Use You to Build His Church

> "I will build my church."
> —MATTHEW 16:18

Are you perfect? You're perfectly wonderful, of course. But do you do absolutely everything right? Absolutely not! Not one of us is perfect. Not even on our very best day.

Peter was certainly not perfect. He shouted when he should have been silent—and was silent when he should have shouted. Peter lost his temper and lost his courage.

The other eleven disciples weren't any better. The truth is, they were just ordinary people. They messed up and made mistakes. But Jesus didn't ask them to be perfect. He asked them to believe and to obey. Because they did, Jesus used those ordinary people to do extraordinary things.

When you choose to believe, He'll use you too. You'll become a part of the church He's promised to build. It's a promise that Jesus first gave to Peter—far-from-perfect Peter—who became Jesus' building stone.

Jesus turned to His disciples and asked them a question: "Who do the people say I am?"

They were standing in the middle of the dust and crowds of Caesarea Philippi. It was a busy place filled with travelers from all over the world. It was a bit wild and a bit crazy, like an ancient Las Vegas and New York City all rolled into one. It was a place where people worshipped phony gods and followed false ways.

Jesus chose that very place to ask His disciples, "Who do the people say I am?"

Jesus could have waited to ask His question until He was back in Galilee, where the crowds loved and adored and cheered for Him. But He didn't.

He could have asked it after He miraculously fed five thousand people or healed the blind and the lame. He would've almost certainly gotten a good answer then. But He didn't.

Jesus chose to ask His question in the wildness of Caesarea Philippi, with all the stuff of the world trying to steal everyone's attention away from Him.

"Who do the people say I am?" He asked.

His disciples looked around at the busy city. Some looked down at their sandals or the ground. Some stroked their beards and stared off into the distance. "Well," they began, "some people say you are John the Baptist. Other people say you are Elijah, or Jeremiah, or maybe one of the prophets."

Then Jesus asked, "Who do *you* say I am?"

Jesus already knew what the world thought of Him, but He most wanted to know what His closest friends thought of Him. After all, they'd been following Him for two years now. They'd seen at least a dozen miracles and heard countless sermons. Did they believe that He was who He said He was?

Simon Peter may have thought for awhile before He said, "You are the Christ, the Son of the living God."

Jesus must have smiled. "You are blessed, Simon," He said. "No one on earth taught you that truth. It was My Father in heaven who showed you who I am. And so, you are Peter (which means *rock*). And I will build My church on this rock."

Peter was not perfect. He made plenty of mistakes. But Peter believed that Jesus truly was the Son of God. And Jesus used that belief to begin building His church.

Peter was an ordinary guy. But he chose to believe the promises of Jesus. One of those promises was given by Jesus when He said, "I will build my church."

There are three beautiful parts to this promise. The first is *who* does the building. Not us, but Jesus. He's in charge, and He never fails.

The second part of the promise is *will*. Jesus didn't say, "I *might* build" or "I *hope* I can build." He said, "I *will* build." Once Jesus starts something, you can count on Him to finish it.

The last part of the promise is about *what* Jesus will build—a church. Jesus' church is simply a gathering of people who believe He truly is the Son of God. Not perfect or problem-free people. But ordinary people who are willing to follow Him. When you believe and follow Him, you also become a stone in the building of His church. You might need a little shaping, a little glue to hold you in place. But . . .

Jesus will use you to build His church.

MY PROMISE TO GOD

I commit to be a part of Jesus' church, and I commit to the truth that unites us: "We believe that Jesus Christ is the Son of God."

Dear Jesus, I'm so thankful I don't have to be perfect to be part of Your church. I just have to agree that You really are the Son of God. Amen.

In Christ you . . . are being built into a place
where God lives through the Spirit.

—EPHESIANS 2:22

———✳———

You are living stones that God is building into his spiritual
temple. What's more, you are his holy priests.

—I PETER 2:5 NLT

———✳———

You should know that you yourselves are God's
temple. God's Spirit lives in you.

—I CORINTHIANS 3:16

———✳———

All of you together are the body of Christ. Each
one of you is a part of that body.

—I CORINTHIANS 12:27

———✳———

Christ, as the Son, is in charge of God's entire house. And we are God's
house, if we keep our courage and remain confident in our hope in Christ.

—HEBREWS 3:6 NLT

———✳———

We will speak the truth in love, growing in every way more and
more like Christ, who is the head of his body, the church.

—EPHESIANS 4:15 NLT

———✳———

You believers are like a building that
God owns. . . . That whole building
is joined together in Christ.

—EPHESIANS 2:20-21

CHAPTER 19

God Will Find You Not Guilty

Those who are in
Christ Jesus are
not judged guilty.

—ROMANS 8:1

Because you are young, there are some things you can't do—at least not yet. You can't vote or drive or jump in a rocket and head for the moon. Not yet. But there's one thing you'll *never* be able to do: you can never save yourself from your sins.

In the beginning, God created us in His own image. To say things He would say. To do things He would do. And sometimes we do. But, often, we don't. We lie, we cheat, we get angry and jealous and selfish. We are guilty of some sort of sin every single day. And it just wouldn't be right if we didn't pay for our wrongs.

God knew we could never pay that price. So Jesus paid it for us. On a cross. So that He could give you this promise: Believe in Him. Follow Him. And you won't be found guilty.

It was decided. Jesus would die.

The Jewish leaders had been waiting for just the right time. And it had finally come.

A bribe and a betrayal, and it was done. Jesus was arrested, given a phony trial, and found guilty. The Jewish leaders tied Him up, led Him away, and turned Him over to Pilate, the Roman governor. They demanded that Jesus die.

Pilate knew an innocent man when he saw one. But when he tried to set Jesus free, the Jewish leaders threatened to start a riot in the streets.

148

So Jesus was sent to the cross. Roman soldiers twisted thorny branches into a crown and shoved it on His head. They beat Him and spit on Him. Then they led Him to Golgotha—the Place of the Skull.

There, the soldiers nailed Jesus' hands and feet to a rough, wooden cross. A sign was placed over His head that read, "THIS IS JESUS, THE KING OF THE JEWS." The soldiers laughed as they rolled dice to see who would get His robe. Then they sat down to watch Him die.

People walking by shouted up at Him, "If You really are the Son of God, come down from that cross! Save Yourself!"

149

Jesus could have done just that. He could have saved Himself. But He didn't. Because there was something He wanted even more. To save His people.

At noon, darkness swept over the land and covered it for three long hours. "My God, my God," Jesus cried out. "Why have You left Me alone?"

The sins of all the world had been placed upon Jesus. And His holy heavenly Father had to turn away.

Some people misunderstood Jesus' words and thought He was calling for Elijah. Someone else ran to fill a sponge with vinegar and lifted it up on a stick for Jesus to drink from.

Jesus cried out, "It is finished." His mission was complete. Jesus bowed His head and died.

In that moment, the earth shook, the dead rose from their graves, and the curtain in the temple—the one that separated the people from the presence of God—was torn in two, from top to bottom.

The centurion, the soldier guarding Jesus, saw all these things and said, "He really was the Son of God!"

It was a dark and terrible day. But it was also the most wonderful of days. Because it was the day Jesus saved His people from their sins.

On that day, Jesus took the punishment that was meant for you. He went to the cross so you—and everyone who chooses to believe in and follow Him—would be found not guilty.

When Jesus died, the temple curtain was torn in two. This curtain stood between the people and God, and it was no thin, delicate thing. It was a wall of fabric as thick as a hand. The fact that it was torn from the *top* to the *bottom* tells us who did the tearing. It wasn't any man. God Himself grabbed the top of that curtain and ripped it in two.

Why? So He could be with you. Because Jesus was punished for your sins, you can live with God. Not just in heaven one day, but in His presence every day.

As a child of God, you don't have to worry about paying for your sins. When you lose your temper, when you tell that little lie, when you're jealous of your friend, Jesus says, "I've already paid for that." He takes away your sins and gives you His perfection. When you tell the world you believe in Jesus and follow Him, He tells all of heaven that you are His child. And He gives you this promise:

You will not be found guilty of your sins.

MY PROMISE TO GOD

I will live every day believing and being thankful that Jesus died so I won't be found guilty of my sins.

Dear God, I'm so sorry for all Jesus suffered on the cross. I know He did that for me. Help me live my whole life saying thank You to Him. Amen.

Christ carried our sins in his body on the cross. He did this
so that we would stop living for sin and start living for what
is right. And we are healed because of his wounds.

—1 PETER 2:24

———*———

God made Christ, who never sinned, to be the offering for our sin,
so that we could be made right with God through Christ.

—2 CORINTHIANS 5:21 NLT

———*———

Christ Jesus came into the world to save sinners.

—1 TIMOTHY 1:15

———*———

This is how God showed his love to us: He sent his only Son into the world
to give us life through him. True love is God's love for us, not our love
for God. God sent his Son to die in our place to take away our sins.

—1 JOHN 4:9–10

———*———

It is your evil that has separated you from your God.
Your sins cause him to turn away from you.

—ISAIAH 59:2

———*———

"I—yes, I alone—will blot out your sins for my own
sake and will never think of them again."

—ISAIAH 43:25 NLT

———*———

You know that Jesus came to take away our
sins, and there is no sin in him.

—1 JOHN 3:5 NLT

CHAPTER 20

GOD'S PROMISE FOR YOU

God Will Erase Death

Death is
destroyed
forever in
victory.

—I CORINTHIANS 15:54

Losing someone you love is hard. Maybe even a little frightening. Perhaps that's because it feels like the end. But what if it weren't the end? What if it were just the beginning of a wonderful new life? What if there's something the Devil doesn't want you to know?

That Friday, when Jesus' body was sealed inside the tomb, His disciples were filled with sadness and fear. Sadness over the loss of their friend, and fear of the death that had taken Him from them. This was not the ending they were expecting, and they worried that the same death might be coming for them. So the disciples of Jesus hid.

But then Sunday came, and their world was made right again. Because Jesus had given His followers a promise. And on Sunday, He kept it. Death couldn't erase Jesus—Jesus erased death! That's the promise He kept for His disciples, and He'll keep it for you too.

It was Sunday morning.

Jesus had died on the cross on Friday. His body was buried in a borrowed tomb. In sadness and fear, His disciples scattered. And Saturday's Sabbath day was long and sad.

But now it was Sunday. The sky was still dark as the Roman soldiers stood guard outside Jesus' tomb. They were there to make sure no one stole His body. To make sure no one could say that this Jesus rose from the dead like He said He would. What a ridiculous thing to say, right?

Wrong.

The soldiers heard a rumble, and the ground began to tremble under their feet. A violent earthquake shook the land as an angel of the Lord flashed down from heaven like a bolt of lightning.

The guards watched him, their eyes wide with fear. The angel boldly strode over to the tomb and to the massive stone that sealed it. Though the stone was almost as tall as a man, he flicked it aside as if it were a pebble.

The guards fainted. And the angel sat down to wait.

The first rays of the morning sun had not yet begun to shine when Mary Magdalene, Mary the mother of James, and the other women headed toward the tomb. They carried spices for Jesus' body. As they walked, they wondered who would roll the stone away for them.

But when they reached the tomb, they saw that the stone had already been rolled away. *No!* Had someone stolen Jesus' body? Then they saw the angel all in white, and they were terrified.

"Don't be afraid," the angel said. "I know you're looking for Jesus, the One who was killed on the cross. But He isn't here. He has risen from death, just as He said He would. Come and see the place where they laid Him. He is not here.

"Now, go and tell the disciples and Peter that Jesus is going to Galilee. You'll see Him there."

The women could hardly believe the wonderful news. Jesus was alive! Not even death could hold their Lord. Jesus had risen from the grave. And that changed everything.

Most importantly, it showed Jesus' disciples that the promise was true: Death cannot defeat Him. And it cannot defeat anyone who follows Him. Death is not the end. For the children of God, it's just the beginning of a glorious new life in heaven with Jesus, our King.

Jesus came to earth with two missions in mind. The first was to defeat sin, and He did that on the cross. The second was to defeat death, which He did on that Sunday morning when the women found His tomb empty.

Sin and death are the Devil's two greatest weapons. He uses sin to make us ashamed and send us running to hide from God. And death? The Devil tries to trick us into thinking that death is the end, so it really doesn't matter how we live.

But Jesus came and took away the power of those weapons. He defeated sin and gave us grace and forgiveness instead. Then, in the ultimate smackdown of the Devil, He defeated death and took away all its power. The empty tomb declared for all time that death is not the end for children of God but is the beginning of life forever with Jesus.

When Jesus rose up out of that grave, He did it to show you the way. He did it to prove that how you live your life does matter. Live it for Him. Because when you do, He promises . . .

God will erase death.

MY PROMISE TO GOD

I trust God has defeated and erased the power of death. It isn't the end; it's the beginning of a new life with Him.

Dear God, thank You for sending Jesus to show me the way to live and the way to get to heaven. I love You, Lord. Amen.

"Those who believe in the Son have eternal life, but those who do not obey the Son will never have life. God's anger stays on them."

—JOHN 3:36 NCV

—✳—

I am sure that nothing can separate us from the love God has for us. Not death, not life, not angels, not ruling spirits, nothing now, nothing in the future, no powers, nothing above us, nothing below us, or anything else in the whole world will ever be able to separate us from the love of God that is in Christ Jesus our Lord.

—ROMANS 8:38-39

—✳—

Jesus said . . . "I am the resurrection and the life. He who believes in me will have life even if he dies. And he who lives and believes in me will never die."

—JOHN 11:25-26

—✳—

This is what God told us: God has given us eternal life, and this life is in his Son. Whoever has the Son has life. But the person who does not have the Son of God does not have life.

—1 JOHN 5:11-12

—✳—

God will raise us from the dead by his power, just as he raised our Lord from the dead.

—1 CORINTHIANS 6:14 NLT

—✳—

God is so rich in mercy, and he loved us so much, that even though we were dead because of our sins, he gave us life when he raised Christ from the dead.

—EPHESIANS 2:4-5 NLT

CHAPTER 21

God Will Turn Your Sadness into Joy

Crying may last
for a night. But
joy comes in
the morning.

—PSALM 30:5

Has anyone ever hurt your feelings? Have things happened that are really sad? Things that don't seem fair? Or have you done things that you wish you had not done? Everyone feels sad sometimes.

However long your tears may last, God has a wonderful promise for you: *"Joy comes in the morning."*

God knows when you're sad, and He understands why you feel the way you do. No matter how much you hurt, He is always right there with you. And if you stay close to God, He will give you a wonderful gift. *Joy.* And that joy will be as bright as the morning when the sun peeks up to say hello, the birds sing, and all feels fresh and new. Your sadness may feel like a dark night, but God promises to bring you a brand-new morning when you will be happy again!

Have you ever needed this promise? Mary Magdalene did. Her tears had lasted through more than one long, lonely night. She needed a new morning to come. It was time for joy.

It was a dark morning. A sad morning.

Mary Magdalene got up before the sun. In the quiet stillness, she set out.

Tears fell down her face. Her feet stumbled over loose pebbles in the path as she made her way to the place where Jesus was buried. She went to the tomb, the tomb of Jesus. As she walked, Mary probably thought about many things. Before she met Jesus, her life was not happy. She was sick and all alone. But then Jesus came. He made her well, and Mary could smile again.

164

Jesus gave Mary her life back. So Mary gave her heart to Jesus.

She listened to Him teach. She watched as He healed sick people, disabled people, and blind people. Wherever Jesus went, Mary followed.

Even to the cross.

On Friday, she had watched as Jesus was nailed to that cross. He died, and her hopes of happiness died with Him.

When they carried His body to the tomb, she followed and watched as a huge stone was rolled over the opening of His tomb to seal it. Surely Mary must have wept and cried through that long, sad Sabbath night and day.

Now it was Sunday, and she had risen early to make her way through the darkness to say one last good-bye to Jesus.

Mary did not think her heart could be any more broken. But she was wrong. She reached the tomb, and a terrible sight was waiting for her. *The stone!* The stone that sealed Jesus' tomb had been rolled away.

Someone robbed the grave and took Jesus' body! Mary thought. She ran back down the path to find Peter and John. "They have taken the Lord out of the tomb," she told them.

Peter and John ran past her to the tomb. John was faster, and he got there first. But Peter was bolder, and he rushed inside. He saw the empty tomb, and he stared at the neatly folded grave clothes. He did not understand.

Then John stepped inside. He saw the empty tomb, and he remembered all that Jesus had said. Jesus told them He would come back to life! Peter and John hurried back to tell the other disciples.

Mary stayed outside the tomb and wept. Her shoulders shook with sobs. And she felt all alone. She looked inside the tomb and saw two angels dressed all in white. They were sitting where Jesus' body had been.

"Woman, why are you crying?" they asked.

Mary thought the angels were only men. After all, no one expects to see angels!

"They have taken away my Lord," she cried. "I don't know where they have put Him." As Mary said these words, she turned away from the tomb and saw Jesus standing there. But she did not know it was Him.

Jesus asked her, "Woman, why are you crying?"

Mary thought He was a gardener. "Did you take Him away, sir?" she asked. "Tell me where you put Him."

Then Jesus said her name, "Mary."

She stopped her crying. *That voice!* She knew that voice. It was Jesus!

Mary Magdalene's sad night of tears ended. It felt like a bright, happy, new morning. Joy came because Jesus came. And she ran to tell the others the good news, the great news, the most joyful news of all: Jesus is alive!

Jesus, the King of all kings, had just risen from the grave. He had beaten Satan and sin and death. He surely had important things to be doing. Disciples to see. People to teach. The sick to heal. But there was one thing Jesus had to do first. He had to keep a promise.

The promise was "Crying may last for a night. But joy comes in the morning." It was time to take away Mary's tears and bring joy to her morning. Jesus took time to comfort Mary Magdalene. Why? Because she was important to Him. And you are too.

The truth is there will be sadness in your life. There will be tears. But Jesus gives you a promise. He kept it for Mary. And He will keep it for you. Your sadness will not last forever . . .

God will turn your sadness to joy.

MY PROMISE TO GOD

When I am sad, I will remember how much Jesus loves me.

Dear Jesus, when I am sad, help me remember that You are with me. Help me trust Your promise, stay close to You, and believe that because I trust in You, joy is coming. Amen.

Those who are sad now are happy. God will comfort them.

—MATTHEW 5:4

———✳———

He will wipe away every tear from their eyes. There will
be no more death, sadness, crying, or pain.

—REVELATION 21:4

———✳———

The Lord will be your light forever. And your time of sadness will end.

—ISAIAH 60:20

———✳———

The joy of the Lord will make you strong.

—NEHEMIAH 8:10

———✳———

I was very worried. But you comforted me and made me happy.

—PSALM 94:19

———✳———

"Now you are sad. But I will see you again and you will
be happy. And no one will take away your joy."

—JOHN 16:22

CHAPTER 22

The Holy Spirit Gives You Power

"The Holy Spirit
will come to
you. Then you
will receive
power."

—ACTS 1:8

Picture a tricycle in your mind. How many wheels does it have? Three, of course! A tricycle with three wheels works great, doesn't it?

Think about that same tricycle again. This time it only has *two* wheels. Do you still want to ride it? *What?* You don't think you would get very far? Why not? You have two perfectly wonderful wheels. Yes . . . but it isn't like a bicycle with two wheels in a line. Your two-wheeled tricycle will be crooked and fall right over. A tricycle won't work the way it's supposed to work without that third wheel.

You wouldn't settle for a tricycle with only two wheels. So don't settle for a faith with only two "wheels." Love God the Father. Follow Jesus the Son. But don't forget about the Holy Spirit.

Do you ever need help doing something—something you know God wants you to do? Maybe it's standing up for someone who's being picked on. Or forgiving a friend who's hurt your feelings. Or talking to someone about Jesus.

Jesus knew that sometimes you would need help to do hard things. That's why He gave this promise: "The Holy Spirit will come to you. Then you will receive power." The Holy Spirit will help you do what God wants you to do.

The Holy Spirit's power was first promised to Jesus' disciples because Jesus knew they would need help to do hard things.

In the city of Jerusalem, the disciples huddled together in one place.

The last few weeks had been like a terrible roller-coaster ride of ups and downs. They had joyfully watched Jesus ride into Jerusalem on the back of a donkey. Great crowds of people had cheered and praised Him.

Then everything changed. Jesus was arrested, beaten, and spat upon. The One who told the storm to be still was nailed to a wooden cross like an ordinary thief. The One who brought Lazarus back to life was killed. And Jesus' body was placed in a borrowed tomb.

Jesus had tried to warn His disciples that this would happen. It was part of God's plan to save them from sin. But they didn't understand. So when all those things *did* happen—just as Jesus had said—they were crushed.

Then everything changed again. The tomb was found empty, and there was so much joy. Jesus was alive! He had risen from the grave! He walked and talked with them. Laughed and ate with them. And taught them once again.

For forty days, Jesus stayed with His followers. Then, in a rush of clouds and glory, He rose up and returned to His home in heaven. Before He left, Jesus gave the disciples a promise: "The Holy Spirit will come to you. Then you will receive power."

Jesus was leaving, but He would not leave His disciples alone. He was sending another to help them. So His disciples watched and prayed and waited.

Suddenly, a great rushing wind roared through the whole house. Flickering flames of fire danced over each disciple's head. And they were each filled with the Holy Spirit of God.

The Helper, the Comforter, the Holy Spirit had come!

The Spirit didn't come to live *beside* them as Jesus had done. Instead, He came to live *inside* them. To guide, to encourage, to pray for them. To give them help and strength. To remind them of all Jesus had taught them. To fill their minds and their mouths with just the right words to tell the world all about Him. And that is exactly what His disciples did.

At that time, people from all over the world were gathered in Jerusalem for the Pentecost celebration. They heard the great rushing noise, and they crowded around the disciples. The disciples began

speaking to the people in their own languages. The Holy Spirit had given them power to speak in languages they had never spoken before!

Then Peter stood up to speak before the whole crowd. This was the same Peter who had been too afraid to tell a servant girl that he even knew Jesus. Now he stood up before thousands and boldly told them all about Jesus—that He was the Son of God. That He had been killed on a cross. That He had risen from the grave. And that He had done all this to save them from their sins.

"Change your hearts and lives," Peter begged the people. "Be baptized, each one of you, in the name of Jesus Christ for the forgiveness of your sins. And you will receive the gift of the Holy Spirit."

Three thousand people believed what Peter said. Three thousand people became followers of Jesus. And three thousand people were given the gift and the power of the Holy Spirit. Because that promise was for them.

And that promise is for you too.

When Jesus left His disciples to return to heaven, He knew they would need help. So the Helper was sent: the Holy Spirit of God.

The Holy Spirit brought the power of God to live inside them. To change them. To help them think like God thinks, love like God loves, and see like God sees. And the Spirit will do the same for you.

The Holy Spirit will also fill your life with His gifts. You've probably heard them called the *fruit* of the Spirit. They are love, joy, peace, patience, kindness, goodness, faithfulness, gentleness, and self-control (Galatians 5:22–23). They grow in your life like apples on the branches of an apple tree. And they'll keep growing in your life as long as you stay connected to the tree—to God.

The Holy Spirit will pray for you, guide you, and give you courage and strength. He will bring the power of God to work in your life. When you follow Jesus, you always have Someone to help you. Because Jesus promised:

The Holy Spirit will come, and you will have power.

MY PROMISE TO GOD

I will ask the Holy Spirit to give me courage to tell others about Jesus and the power to live like Him.

Thank You, God, for sending Your Holy Spirit to help me. Teach me to listen to Him so I will always stay close to You. Amen.

"I will ask the Father, and he will give you another Helper.
He will give you this Helper to be with you forever."

—JOHN 14:16

———✳———

"The Helper is the Spirit of truth. . . . He lives with you and he will be in you."

—JOHN 14:17

———✳———

"The Helper will teach you everything. He will cause you to
remember all the things I told you. This Helper is the Holy
Spirit whom the Father will send in my name."

—JOHN 14:26

———✳———

"When the Spirit of truth comes, he will guide you."

—JOHN 16:13 ESV

———✳———

We do not know how to pray as we should. But the Spirit himself
speaks to God for us, even begs God for us. The Spirit speaks
to God with deep feelings that words cannot explain.

—ROMANS 8:26

———✳———

When you heard the true teaching—the Good News about your salvation—
you believed in Christ. And in Christ, God put his special mark of
ownership on you by giving you the Holy Spirit that he had promised.

—EPHESIANS 1:13 NCV

———✳———

"I will send you the Helper from the Father. He is the Spirit of truth
who comes from the Father. When he comes, he will tell about me."

—JOHN 15:26

CHAPTER 23

GOD'S PROMISE FOR YOU

God Will Meet All Your Needs

My God will use
his wonderful
riches in Christ
Jesus to give
you everything
you need.

—PHILIPPIANS 4:19

Problems. Everyone has them at one time or another. They're just a part of life. Some problems are small and not too tough to handle. But others are big—so big that those problems can start to seem like a prison you can't get out of.

Have you ever felt like a prisoner to your problems? Maybe you just can't escape that mistake you made. Or your fear chains you up and keeps you from trying that thing you really want to do. Maybe it's worries that have you all locked up.

Paul knew a thing or two about being a prisoner. He'd lost his money, his health, and his freedom. But Paul was still happy. How? Because instead of seeing all the things he didn't have, Paul saw all his blessings. And one of the greatest was this promise from God: He will meet all your needs.

from Acts 9

Paul was a prisoner, even though he hadn't done anything wrong. Prisoners aren't usually happy people. So Paul should not have been a happy person, right? Wrong.

Paul *was* happy. He didn't have his freedom, his health, or his money. But he had a secret. He'd learned it long ago, on a dusty road, on his way to Damascus.

Paul had been a very different person back then. Even his name was different: Saul. If there was one name that Christians everywhere trembled to hear, it was *Saul*.

Saul was the most religious man in all Jerusalem. He believed it was his duty as a Jew to stamp out those pesky followers of Christ. Throughout Jerusalem, he had them rounded up, arrested, and even killed.

After a while, though, Saul wasn't happy with just rounding up Christians in Jerusalem. He wanted to take his show on the road. So he headed to the city of Damascus. Just as he was getting close to the city, a bright light shot out of heaven and flashed all around him.

Saul fell to the ground as a voice from heaven said, "Saul, Saul, why do you persecute Me?"

"Who are you?" Saul asked.

"I am Jesus! Now get up," He said. "Go into the city, and there you'll be told what to do."

Saul stood up. But when he opened his eyes, he was blind! The men traveling with him took his hands and led him into the city. For three days, Saul sat in darkness. He didn't eat or drink anything. Until the day Ananias came.

Now, Ananias wasn't thrilled about going to see Saul. After all, Saul had a pretty bad reputation when it came to Christians. And Ananias was a Christian. But God said go, so Ananias went.

Ananias put his hands on Saul's shoulders and said, "Jesus sent me here so that you could see again." Something like scales immediately dropped from Saul's eyes. He could see! He jumped up and was baptized right away.

It wasn't long before Saul—later known as *Paul*—was preaching about Jesus. Then, a few years later, he was off on his first missionary journey. His letters have become part of the Bible. He was beaten, shipwrecked, snake bitten, stoned, and thrown in prison more than once. Through it all, Paul was happy.

All because of the secret he learned on that road to Damascus: Jesus will meet all your needs, especially when you realize that Jesus is all you really need.

On the road to Damascus, Jesus appeared to Saul. What actually happened was that Jesus knocked Saul off his high horse and then left him blind and alone in darkness for three days. Why would Jesus do such a thing? Because Jesus knew that what Saul needed most in his life was a change of direction. So, with a blinding flash of light, Jesus showed up to meet that need. And Saul, the slayer of Christians, was transformed into Paul, the preacher of Christ.

Through Paul, God gives you a promise: He will meet all your needs. Trusting that promise was the secret to Paul's happiness—in spite of being a prisoner, poor, and in pain. Paul *knew* God would take care of Him.

That same promise is yours. When this world causes you pain, when it makes you feel poor and worthless, when it tries to put you in a prison of worry or fear, remember that your God will take care of you. That's His promise:

God will give you everything you need.

MY PROMISE TO GOD

I will trust God to meet all my needs.

Dear God, I know I will have troubles. And I know my life won't always be easy. But I also know that the secret to being happy is to trust You to take care of me. Amen.

I have learned the secret of being happy at any time
in everything that happens. . . . I can do all things
through Christ because he gives me strength.

—PHILIPPIANS 4:12-13

———✳———

The Lord is my shepherd. I have everything I need.

—PSALM 23:1

———✳———

I look to the Lord for help. I wait confidently for God to
save me, and my God will certainly hear me.

—MICAH 7:7 NLT

———✳———

The Lord gives strength to those who are tired. He
gives more power to those who are weak.

—ISAIAH 40:29

———✳———

When they were hungry, you gave them bread from heaven. When
they were thirsty, you brought them water from the rock.

—NEHEMIAH 9:15

———✳———

"You know how to give good things to your children. So surely your heavenly
Father knows how to give the Holy Spirit to those who ask him."

—LUKE 11:13

———✳———

Now that I belong to Christ, I am right with God and this being right
does not come from my following the law. It comes from God through
faith. God uses my faith in Christ to make me right with him.

—PHILIPPIANS 3:9

CHAPTER 24

God Will Right All Your Wrongs

God has decided
on a day that
he will judge
all the world.

—ACTS 17:31

It's a sad fact: sometimes you do things that are wrong. Sometimes it's by accident—you didn't mean to do anything wrong, and you try to make it right. Sometimes it's a mistake that you try to fix. But other times—you might as well admit it—you do the wrong thing on purpose. You lie to get out of trouble. You cheat because you didn't want to study for the test. Or worse—you mean to hurt, and you hurt to be mean. You might even think you're getting away with it! But you're not.

That's because God isn't just sitting around, twiddling His thumbs, and watching you make bad choices. He's giving you a chance to choose Him (2 Peter 3:9). He wants you to choose to obey Him and do what's right by following Jesus. Then, on that day when you meet Him face to face in heaven, God will find you not guilty of all those things you did wrong. *And* He will say, "Well done!" for all those things you did right.

God won't wait forever, though. The day is coming when He will judge you and all the people of the world. That's a promise—and a warning. A warning Paul tried to give to the people of Athens.

Paul walked through the streets of Athens. It was a beautiful city. So full of people—but unfortunately, it was also full of idols to many different gods!

As Paul walked, he also talked. Just as he did everywhere he went—since he'd first met Jesus on that road to Damascus—Paul told the people about his Savior. He spoke to the Jews in the synagogues and to anyone in the marketplace who would listen.

When Paul tried to tell the wise men of Athens about Jesus, they thought he was talking about just another god. After all, they had so many. But they were willing to listen. "Explain this new idea you're teaching," they said. "We've never heard anything like it before."

So Paul began to tell them about God and His Son.

"Men of Athens," he said, "I see that you are very religious. I was walking through your city, and I saw the altars for all the different gods you worship. You even have an altar to 'A God Who Is Not Known.'"

(The people of Athens were very careful with their gods. They didn't want to hurt any god's feelings by leaving him . . . or her . . . or it . . . out!)

"You worship a god you don't even know," Paul said. "That's the God I'm here to tell you about!

"He made the whole world and everything in it. He is Lord of the land and the sky. He doesn't live in temples! And He isn't something you can make from gold or silver or rock.

"This God is the One who gives life, breath, and everything else to people. He wants His people to search for Him. And you can find Him because He is never far away from any of us. Some of your own poets have said: 'For we are his children.' And we are! We are God's children!

"Change your hearts and your lives—worship and follow only Him. Because one day, He will judge all the people of the world. He's already decided what day that will be.

"His Son, Jesus, will be the One to judge us. God chose Jesus long ago. And He proved that Jesus is His Chosen One by raising Him up from the dead! If you believe and follow Him, you will not be found guilty of the wrongs you have done."

When Paul finished, he looked at the people, praying they would believe. Some of them were laughing. *Whoever heard of a man rising from the dead?* Others said, "We'll think about this later. But not today." But some of them *did* believe. And that made Paul—and Jesus—very happy.

There was a reason Paul did all he did. A reason he suffered through beatings and stonings and shipwrecks. He knew a day was coming when God would judge all the people of the world.

Paul also knew that he was a sinner—the worst of sinners, he said. But on the road to Damascus, Jesus had given Paul a second chance. Paul had learned to believe in Jesus. And he spent the rest of his life telling others that they could have that same second chance. You can have it too.

One day, God will judge all the people of the world. Every wrong will be made right. Every sin will be paid for. And those who have chosen to follow Jesus will hear the most wonderful news: "You are Mine. I've already paid for your sins." But those who have chosen to ignore Jesus will hear the terrible news: "Get away from me. . . . I never knew you" (Matthew 7:23). Choose Jesus. Choose Him now. Because He has promised:

God will right all your wrongs.

MY PROMISE TO GOD

I will follow God and trust Him to right all my wrongs.

Dear God, please forgive me for all the times I know what's right and I still do wrong. Thank You for sending Jesus to pay for my sins. Amen.

God wants all people to be saved. And he wants everyone to know the truth. There is only one God. And there is only one way that people can reach God. That way is through Jesus Christ.

—1 TIMOTHY 2:4–5

———✳———

Each of us will have to answer to God for what he has done.

—ROMANS 14:12

———✳———

The Lord is not slow in doing what he promised—the way some people understand slowness. But God is being patient with you. He does not want anyone to be lost. He wants everyone to change his heart and life.

—2 PETER 3:9

———✳———

Do not judge before the right time; wait until the Lord comes. He will bring to light things that are now hidden in darkness. He will make known the secret purposes of people's hearts. Then God will give everyone the praise he should get.

—1 CORINTHIANS 4:5

———✳———

God is fair. He will not forget the work you did and the love you showed for him by helping his people.

—HEBREWS 6:10

———✳———

"The master answered, 'You did well. You are a good servant who can be trusted. You did well with small things. So I will let you care for much greater things. Come and share my happiness with me.'"

—MATTHEW 25:23

CHAPTER 25

God Will Make Everything New

"I am making
everything
new!"

—REVELATION 21:5 NIV

Heaven. People today use that word to describe a lot of things. This dessert is just *heaven*. This park is like *heaven*. What a *heavenly* day!

And it's true—there are some wonderful and beautiful things on this earth. But nothing, no matter how good it is, can compare to the wonders of God's heaven.

Heaven is the home of God. And in heaven you will live in the presence of God for all eternity. What does that mean? It means in heaven there'll never be another moment of darkness or sadness or pain. In heaven there'll never be another tear, another accident, another loss. No more wars, no more crimes, no more saying good-bye to people we love.

In heaven your days will be filled with perfect peace and love and joy. And all of God's creation will be made new. How can we know all this? Because Jesus sent an angel to give His disciple John a glimpse of heaven.

Years had passed since Jesus returned to heaven. But there was still something Jesus wanted His disciple John to see. So He sent an angel to show it to him.

What was it? *Heaven.* The angel opened John's eyes so he could see the home of God.

John watched as the holy city—the New Jerusalem—came down from heaven. Bright and shining like a jewel, it was unlike anything he'd ever seen before.

The angel took out a golden measuring stick and used it to measure the city. It was a square, 1,500 miles wide and 1,500 miles long. Almost as big as the whole country of America! And the city was as tall as it was wide. If it had floors like a skyscraper, it would be more than 600,000 stories tall!

There's plenty of room in heaven.

Then the angel showed John the tree of life. It was so big that it stretched across both sides of the river that flowed through heaven. New fruit filled its branches every month.

There's plenty of food in heaven.

The angel also showed John the twelve gates to the city. On them were written the names of the twelve tribes of Israel. Remember them? They're the ones who tossed Joseph into a pit and sold him as a slave.

197

Then the angel pointed to the
foundations. They were covered with
jewels, and the names of Jesus' first disciples
were written on them. The same disciples who
told the children to leave Jesus alone (Luke 18:15),
who told Jesus to leave the hungry alone (Matthew
14:15), and who left Jesus alone to face the cross
(Matthew 26:56). Not one of them was perfect. They were
sinners. But their names are carved in heaven.
There's plenty of grace in heaven.

But that's not all.

When at last the Devil is completely defeated, then all things will be made new. Everything will be the way God created it to be in the beginning—before the Devil tempted Adam and Eve with that fruit. Before sin.

The wolf and lamb will play together in peace. The leopard will lie down with the goat. Lions won't snarl, and bears won't harm.

God will live with His people. He'll wipe away every tear from their eyes. There will be no more death, sadness, crying, or pain. Because God will make everything new.

Jesus gave John a glimpse of what was to come. A peek into the perfection of heaven. And John wrote it all down so that we could have that same glimpse of the glorious home God has for us. So we can have the hope—the promise—that one day we will live with God.

But *only* if we choose to. You see, heaven is a possibility for everyone, but it is only promised to those who choose to believe in God.

In heaven, Jesus has prepared a place just for you (John 14:3). There are no troubles, and the Lord's light always fills the skies. Heaven will be greater than we can ever imagine. Because God has promised:

He will make everything new.

MY PROMISE TO GOD

I will look forward to heaven more than I look forward to anything on earth.

Dear God, I cannot even imagine how wonderful heaven will be. Thank You for making a place in Your home just for me. Amen.

Your old sinful self has died, and your new life is
kept with Christ in God. Christ is your life, and when
he comes again, you will share in his glory.

—COLOSSIANS 3:3–4 NCV

———✳———

God made a promise to us. And we are waiting for what he
promised—a new heaven and a new earth where goodness lives.

—2 PETER 3:13

———✳———

I will see God. I will see him myself; I will see him with my
very own eyes. How my heart wants that to happen!

—JOB 19:26–27 NCV

———✳———

"After I go and prepare a place for you, I will come back. Then I
will take you to be with me so that you may be where I am."

—JOHN 14:3

———✳———

"Look! I am creating new heavens and a new earth, and no
one will even think about the old ones anymore."

—ISAIAH 65:17 NLT

———✳———

Since you have been raised to new life with Christ, set your sights on
the realities of heaven, where Christ sits in the place of honor at God's
right hand. Think about the things of heaven, not the things of earth.

—COLOSSIANS 3:1–2 NLT

———✳———

Our homeland is in heaven, and we are waiting for our Savior, the Lord
Jesus Christ, to come from heaven. By his power to rule all things, he will
change our humble bodies and make them like his own glorious body.

—PHILIPPIANS 3:20–21 NCV